Tell It Slant

Writing and Shaping Creative Nonfiction

Brenda Miller & Suzanne Paola

McGraw·Hill

New York   Chicago   San Francisco   Lisbon   London   Madrid   Mexico City
Milan   New Delhi   San Juan   Seoul   Singapore   Sydney   Toronto

Library of Congress Cataloging-in-Publication Data

Miller, Brenda.
    Tell it slant : writing and shaping creative nonfiction / by Brenda Miller and
Suzanne Paola.
        p.   cm.
    Includes bibliographical references.
    ISBN 0-07-144494-7
      1. English language—Rhetoric.   2. Journalism—Authorship.   3. Investigative
reporting.   4. Creative writing.   5. Report writing.   I. Paola, Suzanne.
II. Title.

PE1408.M548   2004b
808'.042—dc22   2004008443

12 DSH/DSH   3 2 1 0

ISBN 0-07-144494-7

Emily Dickinson poem (p. iii) reprinted by permission of the publishers and the trustees of
Amherst College from *The Poems of Emily Dickinson*, Thomas H. Johnson, ed., Cambridge:
Mass.: The Belknap Press of Harvard University Press, copyright © 1951, 1955, 1979,
1983 by the president and fellows of Harvard College.

This book is printed on acid-free paper.

Tell all the Truth but tell it Slant—
Success in Circuit lies
Too bright for our infirm Delight
The Truth's superb surprise
As Lightening to the Children eased
With explanation kind
The Truth must dazzle gradually
Or every man be blind—

—EMILY DICKINSON

Contents

Introduction

Where to Begin

The word is the making of the world.
— WALLACE STEVENS

Here's how it happens: I'm at a party, or sitting quietly in my seat on an airplane, or milling around at a family reunion, and someone finally asks me the question: "So, you're a writer. What do you write?" It's a deceptively simple question. And seems to demand a simple response.

    But in the split second before I can answer, I go through all the possible replies in my head. "Well," I could say, "I write essays." But essays sound too much like academic papers and articles. I could say, simply, "Nonfiction," but then they might think I write celebrity biographies, cookbooks, or historical treatises on World War II. I could try to take the easy way out and say I write autobiography or memoir, but people would raise their eyebrows and say, "Memoir? Aren't you too young to write your memoirs?" Besides, not all of what I write is memoir; in fact, many of my pieces are not based in private memory at all.

    *All this is too much for casual party chat. I need a term that, once deployed, will answer all their questions for good. But I know that if I answer with the correct phrase—*creative nonfiction*—I'm in for a long night. My interrogator will warm up to the debate, throwing out the opening volley: "Creative nonfiction? Isn't that an oxymoron?" His forehead crinkles, and his eyes search my own, trying to understand what, exactly, I'm talking about.*

I want to tell him that I love writing creative nonfiction precisely because of this ambiguity. I love the way writing creative nonfiction allows me to straddle a kind of "borderland" where I can discover new aspects of myself and the world, forge surprising metaphors, and create artistic order out of life's chaos. I'm never bored when I write in this genre, always jazzed by the new ways I can stretch my writing muscles. But I rarely trust my listener will understand. So, more often than not, I smile and say, "Maybe I'll show you sometime." Then I execute a pirouette and turn his attention toward the view out the window or to the lovely fruit punch in its cut-glass bowl. I direct his attention to the myriad things of this world, and maybe that is the correct answer after all.

—BRENDA

When Emily Dickinson wrote, "Tell all the Truth but tell it Slant / Success in Circuit lies . . ." what did she mean by these lines? We think she meant that truth takes on many guises; the truth of art can be very different from the truth of day-to-day life. Her poems and letters, after all, reveal her deft observation of the outer world, but it is "slanted" through the poet's distinctive vision. We chose her poem as both title and epigraph for this book because it so aptly describes the task of the creative nonfiction writer: to tell the truth, yes, but to become more than a mere transcriber of life's factual experiences.

Every few years, National Public Radio checks in on a man who feels compelled to record every minute of his day in a diary. As you can imagine, the task is gargantuan and ultimately imprisons him. He becomes a slave to this recording act and can no longer function in the world. The transcription he leaves may be a comprehensive and "truthful" one, but it remains completely unreadable; after all, who cares to read reams and reams of such notes? What value do they hold apart from the author? In nonfiction, if we place a premium on fact, then this man's diary would be the ultimate masterpiece. But in literature and art, we applaud style, meaning, and effect over the bare facts. We go to literature—and perhaps especially creative nonfiction literature—to learn not about the author, but about ourselves; we want to be *moved* in some way. That emotional resonance happens only through skillful use of artistic techniques. As Salman Rushdie put it, "Literature is where I go to explore the highest and lowest places in human society and in the human spirit, where I hope to find not absolute truth but the truth of the tale, of the imagination and of the heart."

Simply by choosing to write in this genre, and to present your work as non-fiction, you make an artistic statement. You're saying that the work is rooted in the "real" world. Though the essay might contain some elements of fabrication, it is directly connected to you as the author behind the text. There is a truth to it that you want to claim as your own, a bond of trust between reader and writer. If you present a piece as fiction, you are saying that the work is rooted in the world of the imagination. Though the story may contain autobiographical elements, the reader cannot assume that it has a direct bearing on the truth of the writer's life or experience. At some point, every writer needs to decide how she wants to place herself in relationship to the reader; the choice of genre establishes that relationship and the rules of engagement.

The more you read and study, the more you will discover that creative non-fiction assumes a particular, creating *self* behind the nonfiction prose. When you set about to write creative nonfiction about any subject, you bring to this endeavor a strong voice and a singular vision. This voice must be loud and interesting enough to be heard among the noise coming at us in everyday life. If you succeed, you and the reader will find yourself in a close, if not intimate, relationship that demands honesty and a willingness to risk a kind of exposure you may never venture in face-to-face encounters.

This is not to say that creative nonfiction must be "self-centered." On the contrary, creative nonfiction often focuses on material outside the life of the author, and it certainly need not use a personal "I" speaker. It's the "creative" part of the term *creative nonfiction* that means a single, active imagination is behind the piece of reality this author will unfold. Essayist Scott Russell Sanders wrote, "Feeling overwhelmed by data, random information, the flotsam and jetsam of mass culture, we relish the spectacle of a single consciousness making sense of a portion of the chaos. . . . The essay is a haven for the private, idiosyncratic voice in an era of anonymous babble."

This "idiosyncratic voice" uses all the literary devices available to fiction writers and poets—vivid images, scenes, metaphors, dialogue, satisfying rhythms of language, and so forth—while still remaining true to experience and the world. Or, as novelist and essayist Cynthia Ozick put it, "Like a poem, a genuine essay is made out of language and character and mood and temperament and pluck and chance."

Creative nonfiction can focus on either private experience or public domain, but in either case, the inner self provides the vision and the shaping influence to infuse the work with this sense of "pluck and chance." In many cases, the essayist may find himself "thinking aloud" on the page. Then the essay becomes a continual process of unexpected discovery. The creative nonfiction writer continually chooses to question and expand his or her own limited perceptions.

Lee Gutkind, who edits the journal *Creative Nonfiction*, says creative nonfiction "heightens the whole concept and idea of essay writing." He has come up with the "the five Rs" of creative nonfiction: Real Life, Reflection, Research, Reading, and 'Riting. That second "R," Reflection, means that in contrast to traditional objective journalism, creative nonfiction allows for and encourages "a writer's feelings and responses . . . as long as what [writers] think is written to embrace the reader in a variety of ways." Imagination coupled with facts form this hybrid genre that is both so exciting and so challenging to write.

As in any creative enterprise, the most difficult challenge to writing creative nonfiction lies in knowing where to begin. One might think that creative nonfiction would provide an easy out for this question. After all, someone might chide, all the material is at your fingertips. It's nonfiction after all; the world is yours for the taking. But the minute creative nonfiction writers put pen to paper, they realize a truth both invigorating and disheartening: we are not the rote recorder of life experience. We are artists creating artifice. And as such, we have difficult choices to make every step of the way.

Memoir may seem more straightforward, but as William Zinsser articulates in his introduction to *Inventing the Truth: The Art and Craft of Memoir*, "Good memoirs are a careful act of construction. We like to think that an interesting life will simply fall into place on the page. It won't. . . . Memoir writers must manufacture a text, imposing narrative order on a jumble of half-remembered events."

We've designed this book to help you gain access to your particular stories and memories—your particular voice—while also providing suggestions for turning your gaze onto the world in a way that will allow you to find material outside of the self. We begin with memory and move steadily outward to family, environment, spirituality, history, the arts, and the world. In this way, we hope you will begin to consider both your individual life and our collective lives as material for creative nonfiction. Readers will want to read your work not because they wish to lend a sympathetic ear to a stranger, but because of the way your truth-filled stories may illuminate their own lives and perceptions of the world.

At the end of each chapter, we provide a series of "Try It" exercises. These are prompts to help you put into action the principles we've explained. Use them as starting points to creating your own brand of creative nonfiction.

PART 1

UNEARTHING YOUR MATERIAL

Remember that the writers whom we call eternal or simply good and who intoxicate us have one common and very important characteristic: they get somewhere, and they summon you there, and you feel, not with your mind, but with your whole being, that they have a certain purpose and, like the ghost of Hamlet's father, do not come and excite the imagination for nothing. He who desires nothing, hopes for nothing, and is afraid of nothing, cannot be an artist.

—ANTON CHEKHOV, IN A LETTER TO
ALEXEI SUVORIN, NOV. 25, 1892

1

The Body of Memory

Memory begins to qualify the imagination, to give it another
formation, one that is peculiar to the self. . . . If I were to remember
other things, I should be someone else.

           —N. Scott Momaday

*In my earliest memory, I'm a four-year-old girl waking slowly from anes-
thesia. I lift my head off the damp pillow and gaze blearily out the bars of
my hospital crib. I can see a dim hallway with a golden light burning; somehow I know in that hallway my mother will appear any minute now, bearing ice cream and 7-Up. She told me as much before the operation: "All good
girls get ice cream and 7-Up when their tonsils come out," she said, stroking
my hair. "It's your reward for being brave." I'm vaguely aware of another
little girl screaming for her mother in the crib next to mine, but otherwise
the room remains dark and hushed, buffered by the footfalls of nurses who
stop a moment at the doorway and move on.*

* I do not turn to face my neighbor, afraid her terror will infect me; I can
feel the tickling urge to cry burbling up in my wounded throat, and that
might be the end of me, of all my purported bravery and the promised ice
cream. I keep my gaze fixed on that hallway, but something glints in my
peripheral vision and I turn to face the bedside table. There, in a mason
jar, my tonsils float. They rotate in the liquid: misshapen ovals, pink and
nubbly, grotesque.*

* And now my mother has simply appeared, with no warning or an-
nouncement. Her head leans close to the crib, and she gently plies the spoon*

*between the bars, places it between my lips, and holds it there while I swal-
low. I keep my gaze fixed on her face, and she keeps her gaze on mine,
though I know we're both aware of those tonsils floating out of reach. The
nurses pad about, and one of them enters the room bearing my "Badge of
Courage." It's a certificate with a lion in the middle surrounded by laurels,
my name scripted in black ink below. My mother holds it out to me, through
the bars, and I run a finger across my name, across the lion's mane, across
the dry yellowed parchment.*

—BRENDA

The Earliest Memory

What is your earliest memory? What is the memory that always emerges from
the dim reaches of your consciousness as the *first one*, the beginning to this
life you call your own? Most of us can pinpoint them, these images that
assume a privileged station in our life's story. Some of these early memories
have the vague aspect of a dream, some the vivid clarity of a photograph. In
whatever form they take, they tend to exert on us a mysterious fascination.

Memory itself could be called its own bit of creative nonfiction. We continually—often unconsciously—renovate our memories, shaping them into
stories that bring coherence to chaos. Memory has been called the ultimate
"mythmaker," continually seeking meaning in the random and often unfath-
omable events in our lives. "A myth," writes John Kotre, author of *White
Gloves: How We Create Ourselves Through Memory,* "is not a falsehood but a
comprehensive view of reality. It's a story that speaks to the heart as well as
the mind, seeking to generate conviction about what it thinks is true."

The first memory then becomes the starting point in our own narratives
of the self. "Our first memories are like the creation stories that humans have
always told about the origins of the earth," Kotre writes. "In a similar way,
the individual self—knowing how the story is coming out—selects its earliest memories to say, 'This is who I am because this is how I began.'" As writers, we naturally return again and again to these beginnings and scrutinize
them. By paying attention to the illogical, unexpected details, we just might
light upon the odd yet precise images that help our lives make sense, at least
long enough for our purposes as writers.

The prominent fiction writer and essayist David James Duncan calls such autobiographical images "river teeth." Using the image of knots of dense wood that remain in a river years after a fallen tree disintegrates, Duncan creates a metaphor of how memory, too, retains vivid moments that stay in mind long after the events that spurred them have been forgotten. He writes:

> *There are hard, cross-grained whorls of memory that remain inexplicably lodged in us long after the straight-grained narrative material that housed them has washed away. Most of these whorls are not stories, exactly: more often they're self-contained moments of shock or of inordinate empathy. . . . These are our "river teeth"—the time-defying knots of experience that remain in us after most of our autobiographies are gone.*

Virginia Woolf had her own term for such "shocks" of memory. She calls them "moments of being" and they become essential to our very sense of self. They are the times when we get jolted out of our everyday complacency to really *see* the world and all that it contains. This shock-receiving capacity is essential for the writer's disposition. "I hazard the explanation," she writes, "that a shock is at once in my case followed by the desire to explain it. . . . I make it real by putting it into words." Woolf's early moments of being, the vivid first memories from childhood, are of the smallest, most ordinary things: the pattern of her mother's dress, for example, or the pull cord of the window blind skittering across the floor of their beach house.

The memories that can have the most emotional impact for the writer are those we don't really understand, the images that rise up before us quite without our volition. For example, the flash of our mother's face as she sips from a cooled cup of coffee, her eyes betraying some private grief you've never seen before; or the smell of grapefruit ripening on a tree outside your bedroom window. Perhaps the touch of a stranger's hand reminds you of the way your grandmother casually grasped your hand in her own, the palm so soft but the knuckles so rough, as you sat together watching television, not speaking a word.

These are the river teeth, or the moments of being, the ones that suck your breath away. What repository of memory do you hold in your heart rather than your head? What are the pictures that rise up to the surface without your bidding? Take these as your cue. Pick up your pen, your net, your magnet, whatever it takes. Be on alert. This is where you begin.

Metaphorical Memory

A metaphor is a way at getting at a truth that exists beyond the literal. By pinpointing certain images as *symbolic*, writers can go deeper than surface truths and create essays that work on many levels at once. This is what writers are up to all the time, not only with memory but with the material of experience and the world. We resurrect the details to describe not only the surface appearance, but also to make intuitive connections, to articulate some truth that cannot be spoken of directly.

Many writers allow early memories to "impress themselves" on the mind. They do not dismiss them as passing details but rather probe them for any insights they may contain. They ask not only "what?" but "why?" "Why do I remember the things I do? Why these memories and not others?"

Let's go back to that first memory of the tonsils, that early river tooth in the personal essay at the beginning of this chapter. For me, Brenda, as a writer it is not important *what* I remember—or even the factual accuracy of the scene—but *why* I recall it the way I do. And, I keep coming back to that incongruous jar of tonsils. I doubt the doctors did such a thing (my mother has no recollection of it), but it remains the most stubborn and intractable part of the scene. What I like about this part of my memory is its very illegibility. The best material cannot be deciphered in an instant, with a fixed meaning that, once pinned down, remains immutable. No. As essayists, we want the rich stuff, the inscrutable images whose meaning is never clear at first, second, or third glance.

I could interpret that jar of tonsils in any number of ways, but this is the one I light on most frequently. When I woke from having my tonsils removed, I knew for the first time that my body was not necessarily a whole unit, always intact. At that moment, I understood the courage that it will take to bear this body into a world that will most certainly cause it harm. Of course, as a child I realized no such thing. But, as an adult—*as a writer preserving this memory in language*—I begin to create a metaphor that will infiltrate both my writing and my sense of self from here on out.

Think back on that early memory of yours, the one that came to mind instantly. Illuminate the details, shine a spotlight on them until they begin to yield a sense of truth revealed. Where is your body in this memory? What kind of language does it speak? What metaphor does it offer for you to puzzle out in writing?

Muscle Memory

The body, memory, and mind exist in sublime interdependence, each part wholly twined with the others. There is a phrase used in dancing, athletics, parachuting, and other fields that require sharp training of the body: *muscle memory*. Once the body learns the repetitive gestures of a certain movement or skill, the memory of how to execute these movements will be encoded in the muscles. That is why, for instance, we never forget how to ride a bike. Or why, years after tap dance lessons, one can still execute a convincing shuffle-hop-step across a kitchen floor.

One cannot speak of memory—and of bodily memory in particular—without trotting out Marcel Proust and his famous madeleine. Proust dips his cookie in the lime-blossom tea, and *Remembrance of Things Past* springs forth, all six volumes of it. Because memory is so firmly fixed in the body, it takes an object that appeals to the senses to dislodge memory and allow it to float freely into the mind or onto the page. *These* memories will have resonance precisely because they have not been forced into being by a mind insistent on fixed meanings. It is the body's story and so one that resonates with a sense of an inadvertent truth revealed. As writer Terry Tempest Williams has said, the most potent images and stories are those that "bypass rhetoric and pierce the heart."

So, as far as memory devices go, you could do worse than turn to the body for guidance. The body can offer an inexhaustible store of triggers to begin any number of essays, each of which will have greater significance than what appears on the surface. Sometimes, what matters to us most is what has mattered to the body. Memory may pretend to live in the cerebral cortex, but it requires muscle—real muscle—to animate it again for the page.

The Five Senses of Memory

By paying attention to the sensory gateways of the body, you also begin to write in a way that naturally *embodies* experience, making it tactile for the reader. Readers tend to care deeply only about those things they *feel* in the body at a visceral level. And so as a writer consider your vocation as that of a translator: one who renders the abstract into the concrete. We experience the world through our senses. We must translate that experience into the language of the senses as well.

Smell

"Smell is a potent wizard that transports us across thousands of miles and all the years we have lived," wrote Helen Keller in her autobiography. "The odors of fruits waft me to my southern home, to my childhood frolics in the peach orchard. Other odors, instantaneous and fleeting, cause my heart to dilate joyously or contract with remembered grief."

Though Helen Keller's words are made more poignant by the fact that she was blind and deaf, we all have this innate connection to smell. Smell seems to travel to our brains directly, without logical or intellectual interference. Physiologically, we *do* apprehend smells more quickly than the other sensations, and the images aroused by smell act as beacons leading to our richest memories, our most private selves. Smell is so intimately tied up with *breath*, after all, a function of our bodies that works continually, day and night, keeping us alive. And so smell keys us into the memories that evoke the continual ebb and flow of experience. The richest smells can be the most innocent: the smell of a Barbie doll; Play-Doh; the house right after your mother has cleaned (the hot dust inside the vacuum, the tart scent of Lemon Pledge); or the shoes in your father's closet, redolent of old polish. Or, the smells can be more complex: the aftershave your father wore the day he lost his job or the scent of your baby's head when you first held her in your arms.

What are the smells you remember that even in memory make you stop a moment and breathe deeply, or that make your heart beat more vigorously, your palms ache for what's been lost? Write these down. Write as quickly as you can, seeing how one smell leads to another. What kinds of image, memories, or stories might arise from this sensory trigger?

Taste

Food is one of the most social gifts we have. The bond between mother and child forms over the feeding of that child, either at the breast or at the bottle, the infant body held close, the eyes intent on the parent's face. When you sit down to unburden yourself to a friend, you often do so over a meal prepared together in the kitchen, the two of you chopping vegetables or sipping wine as you articulate whatever troubles have come to haunt you. When these predicaments grow overwhelming, we turn to comfort food, meals that spark in us a memory of an idealized, secure childhood. When we are falling in love, we offer food as our first timid gesture toward intimacy.

In his famous essay "Afternoon of an American Boy," E. B. White vividly remembers the taste of cinnamon toast in conjunction with the first stumbling overtures of a boyhood crush. In "A Thing Shared," food aficionado M. F. K. Fisher uses something as simple and commonplace as the taste of a peach pie—"the warm round peach pie and cool yellow cream"—to describe a memory of her father and sister the first time they found themselves alone without the mediating influence of their mother. The food acts as more than mere sustenance; it becomes a moment of communion. "That night I not only saw my father for the first time as a person. I saw the golden hills and the live oaks as clearly as I have ever seen them since; and I saw the dimples in my little sister's fat hands in a way that still moves me because of that first time; and I saw food as something beautiful to be shared with people instead of as a thrice-daily necessity." This scene becomes an illustration of how we awaken to one another. It's less about her own family than about the fleeting moments of connection that can transpire in *all* families, in one way or another.

What are the tastes that carry the most emotion for you? The tastes that, even in memory, make you stop a moment and run your tongue over your lips and swallow hard? Write these down, as quickly as you can. Which scenes, memories, associations come to the surface?

Hearing

Sounds often go unnoticed. Because we cannot consciously cut off our hearing unless we plug our ears, we've learned to filter sounds, picking and choosing the ones that are important, becoming inured to the rest. But these sounds often make up a subliminal backdrop to our lives, and even the faintest echo can tug back moments from the past in their entirety.

For example, in his short gem of an essay, "The Fine Art of Sighing," memoirist Bernard Cooper uses a sound as subtle as a sigh to elucidate his relationship to his family, himself, and the world. He describes how his father sighs, how his mother sighs, and how he, himself, sighs. And, paradoxically, by focusing in on this small, simple act, Cooper is able to reveal much larger things: his mother's dissatisfaction with domestic life, his father's gruff sensual nature, and Cooper's ambivalence about his own body and sexuality. "A friend of mine once mentioned that I was given to long and ponderous sighs. Once I became aware of this habit, I heard my father's sighs in my own and knew for a moment his small satisfactions. At other times, I felt my mother's restlessness and wished I could leave my body with my breath, or be happy in the body my breath left behind."

Music is not so subtle but rather acts as a blaring soundtrack to our emotional lives. Think about the bonds you formed with friends over common musical passions, the days spent listening to the same song over and over as you learned the mundane yet painful lessons of love. Sometimes you turned up that song as loud as you could so that it might communicate to the world—and to your deepest, deafest self—*exactly* the measure of your emotion.

We often orchestrate our memories around the music that accompanied those pivotal eras of our lives. In his essay "A Voice for the Lonely," Stephen Corey writes movingly about how a certain Roy Orbison song can always call him back to his sophomore year of high school, to his friendship with a boy as outcast as himself. He characterizes those moments as "The right singer, the right sadness, the right silence." When you have the soundtrack down, the rest of life seems to fall into place.

Touch

Hospitals rely on volunteers to hold babies on the infant wards. Their only job is to hold and rock any baby that is crying or in distress. The nurses, of course, do not have time for such constant care, but they know this type of touch is essential as medicine for their patients' healing. As we grow, this need for touch does not diminish, and thus our raging desires for contact, our subtle and not-so-subtle maneuvers that lead us into skin-to-skin encounters with other living beings.

We are constantly aware of our bodies, of how they feel as they move through the world. Without this sense we become lost, disoriented in space and time. And the people who have affected us the most are the ones who have *touched* us in some way, who have reached beyond this barrier of skin and made contact with our small, isolated selves.

Sometimes an essayist can focus on the tactile feel of objects as a way to explore deeper emotions or memories. For instance, in his short essay "Buckeye," Scott Russell Sanders focuses on the feel of the buckeye seeds that his father carried with him to ward off arthritis. They are "hollow," he says, "hard as pebbles, yet they still gleam from the polish of his hands." Sanders then allows the sensation of touch to be the way we get to know his father:

> *My father never paid much heed to pain. Near the end, when his worn knee often slipped out of joint, he would pound it back in place with a rubber mallet. If a splinter worked into his flesh beyond the reach of tweezers, he would heat the blade of his knife over a cigarette lighter and slice through the skin.*

Such sensory details bring the reader almost into the father's body, feeling the pound of that mallet, the slice of the skin. He never needs to tell us his father was a tough man; the images do all the work for him. These details also allow us to see the narrator, Sanders, watching his father closely, and so this scene also conveys at least a part of their relationship and its emotional tenor.

Think about the people in your life who have touched you deeply. What was the quality of their physical touch on your body? How did they touch the objects around them? Why do you think this touch lingers in memory?

Sight

How do you see the world? How do you see yourself? Even linguistically, our sense of sight seems so tied up in our perceptions, stance, opinions, personalities, and knowledge of the world. To see something often means to finally understand, to be enlightened, to have our vision cleared. What we choose to see—and *not* to see—often says more about us than anything else.

When we "look back" in memory, we *see* those memories. Our minds have catalogued an inexhaustible storehouse of visual images. Now the trick is for you to render those images in writing. Pay attention to the smallest details: the way a tree limb cuts its jagged edge against a winter sky or the dull canary yellow of the bulldozer that leveled your favorite house on the street. Close your eyes to see these images more clearly. Trace the shape of your favorite toy or the outline of a beloved's face. Turn up the lights in the living room. Go out walking under a full moon. Keep looking.

For Annie Dillard, in her jubilant essay "Seeing" (from *Pilgrim at Tinker Creek*), being able to see truly is akin to spiritual awakening:

One day I was walking along Tinker Creek thinking of nothing at all and I saw the tree with the lights in it. I saw the backyard cedar where the mourning doves roost charged and transfigured, each cell buzzing with flame. . . . It was less like seeing than like being for the first time seen, knocked breathless by a powerful glance. . . . I had been my whole life a bell, and never knew it until at that moment I was lifted and struck.

What are the moments in your life that have "struck" you? How have they been engraved in memory?

Fortunately, we live in an age where visual memories are routinely preserved in photographs and on videotape. Sometimes these photos and films can act not only as triggers for your memory—reminding you of the visual details of the experience—but they can also prompt you to delve more deeply below the surface.

TRY IT

1. Write a scene of a very early, vivid memory. What calls out for further examination? Are you realistic? What are the odd details, the ones that don't seem to fit with other people's versions of the story? What in this scene seems to matter to you? Should it? What are you leaving out? If you get stuck, keep repeating the phrase "I remember" to start off your sentences; allow this rhythm to take you further than you thought you could go.

> VARIATION 1: Do you have an ideal "earliest memory"? Write this out, and see how your imagination and your memory intersect or diverge. Is there an essay in the process of memory itself?

> VARIATION 2: Talk with family members about *their* memories of the time you pinpoint as your first memory. How do they corroborate or deny your own memory? How can you create a "collaborative" memory that includes their versions of the events? How does this memory enact a family "myth"? Is there an essay about the way these divergent accounts work together?

2. In the preface to his anthology *The Business of Memory*, Charles Baxter writes, "What we talk about when we talk about memory is—often—what we

have forgotten and what has been lost. The passion and torment and significance seem to lie in that direction." What have you forgotten in your life? What are the moments that keep sliding out of reach? Write for twenty minutes, using the phrase "I can't remember" to start off each sentence. Where does such an examination lead you?

You may find that by using this exercise you can back into the scenes and images you *do* remember but never knew how to approach. You can write some very powerful essays based on this prompt, exploring material that seemed too dangerous to examine head-on.

> VARIATION: After you've lighted on some events or times you can't fully articulate, do a little research. Ask others about their memories of that time. Find documents or photographs that may shed some light on the issue. Be a detective, looking for clues. After you've gathered enough evidence, write an essay that focuses on the way your memory and the "reality" either differ or coincide. Why have you forgotten the things you did?

3. How many different "firsts" can you remember in your life? The first meal you remember enjoying, the first smell you remember wanting to smell again, the first day of school, the first book you remember reading by yourself, the first album you ever bought, the first time you drove a car, the first kiss, the first time you were touched in a sexual way? How does your memory of these "first" events color your perception of yourself? What kinds of metaphors do they generate for your life story?

Smell
1. Gather articles that you know carry some smell that is evocative for you. One by one, smell them deeply, and then write the images that arise in your mind. Write quickly, allowing the smell to trigger other sensory associations.

2. Which smells in your life are gone for you now? Which ones would you give anything to smell again? Have you ever been "ambushed" by a smell you didn't expect? For example, have you opened a box of clothing from a deceased relative and had the smell of that person's house flood over you? Or, have you walked into a friend's house and smelled a meal exactly like one you remember from

childhood? Write a scene about such an incident. If you can't remember anything like that, imagine one. How do these sensory memories differ from memories of the past you'd normally conjure up? Write an essay exploring the idea that your body carries its own dormant memories.

> VARIATION FOR A GROUP: Each person brings in an object that carries some kind of strong smell and takes a turn being the leader. Keep the object hidden until it is your turn. The rest of the group members close their eyes while the leader brings this object to each person and asks him or her to smell deeply. After everyone has had a chance, the leader hides the object again. Each person immediately writes the images and associations that smell evoked. Share these writings with each other and see how similarly or differently you reacted to the same odor.

Taste

1. Try to remember the first meal you consciously tasted and enjoyed. Describe this meal in detail; make yourself hungry with these details. Who ate this meal with you? If you can't remember any such meal, imagine one.

2. If you were to write a life history through food, what would be the "touch-stone" moments, the meals that represented turning points for you? Which meals have you loved? Which meals have you hated? Which meals marked important transitions in your life?

> VARIATION FOR A GROUP: Have "food exploration" days set aside for your group meetings. On these days, one person is responsible for bringing in an item of food for everyone to taste. Try to choose foods that leave strong sensory impressions: a mango, perhaps, or a persimmon. After exploring the sight, textures, and smells, taste it. Describe this food in detail, then go on to whichever images and metaphorical associations arise. In your own life, what is most like a mango? Begin an essay by outlining which people, feelings, events, or memories this food conjures up for you and why.

Touch

1. Take an inventory of the scars or marks on your body. How were they received? How do these external scars relate to any internal "markings" as well?

2. Find an object that you consider a talisman, something you either carry with you or keep in a special place in your home. Hold it in your hand, and, with your eyes closed, feel all its textures. Begin to write, using this tactile description to trigger memories, scenes, and metaphors.

> VARIATION FOR A GROUP: Each person brings in such an object for a "show-and-tell," explaining the story behind the item. Pass these things around the room for everyone to examine, and then write based on *someone else's* talisman. What did it feel like in your hand? How does it trigger memories of your own?

Sound

1. Try re-creating a scene from your childhood using *only* the sense of hearing. What music is playing in the background? Whose voice is on the radio? How loud is the sound of traffic? What do the trees sound like in the wind? Are there insects, birds, animals? A hum from a factory? Rain, rivers, the lapping of a lake? What is the quality of the silence? Try to pick out as many ambient sounds as you can, then begin to amplify the ones you think have the most metaphorical significance. What kind of emotional tone do these sounds give to the piece?

2. Put on a piece of music that you strongly associate with a certain era of your life. Using this music as a soundtrack, zero in on a particular scene that arises in your mind. Try writing the scene *without mentioning the music at all*, but through your word choices and imagery and sentence structure convey the essence of this music's rhythm and beat.

> VARIATION: Do the same thing, but this time use fragments of the lyrics as "scaffolding" for the essay. Give us a few lines, then write part of the memory those lines evoke in you. Give us a few more, and continue with the memory, so that the song plays throughout the entire piece.

> VARIATION FOR A GROUP: Each person brings in a tape or CD of instrumental music that evokes some kind of strong emotion. Put on these pieces in turn, and have everybody write for at least five minutes to each track, trying not to describe the music directly but focusing instead on the images and memories the music brings up. Choose a few to read aloud when you're done, but don't mention which piece of music acted as the trigger; have the rest of the group try to guess which music corresponds to which writing.

Sight

1. What do you see when you look in the mirror? Where does your gaze land first? How does this gaze determine your attitude toward yourself and your life? Do you see your younger self beneath the present-day face? Can you determine your future self through this gaze?

2. Using a photograph of yourself, a relative, or a friend, describe every detail of the scene. Then focus in on one object or detail that seems unexpected to you in some way. How does this detail trigger specific memories? Also, imagine what occurred just before and just after this photograph was taken; what is left outside the frame? For instance, write an essay with a title such as "After [Before] My Father Is Photographed on the *U.S.S. Constitution*." (Insert whichever subject is appropriate for the photographs you've chosen.)

VARIATION FOR A GROUP: Repeat the above exercise, but then trade photographs with your neighbor. Which details strike you? How does any part of the scene remind you of scenes from your own life? Perform a number of these trades around the room to see which details leap up from other people's photographs.

2

Writing the Family

One thing that we always assume, wrongly, is that if we write about people honestly they will resent it and become angry. If you come at it for the right reasons and you treat people as you would your fictional characters . . . if you treat them with complexity and compassion, sometimes they will feel as though they've been honored, not because they're presented in some ideal way but because they're presented with understanding.

—KIM BARNES, AUTHOR OF *IN THE WILDERNESS*
AND *HUNGRY FOR THE WORLD*

My brother is swinging the bat and I'm bored in the stands, seven years old. My mother has given me a piece of paper and a pen that doesn't have much ink in it. I've written, "I HAVE TWO BROTHERS. ONE IS A LITTLE ONE. ONE IS A BIG ONE. WE ONLY HAVE TWO GIRLS IN OUR FAMILY. ONE IS ME. ONE IS MY MOTHER." The mothers sit all around me, their straight skirts pulled tight across their knees. My brother is swinging the bat and wiggling his hips on the other side of the mesh. "THE BIG BROTHER IS MEAN. THE LITTLE BROTHER IS SOMETIMES MEAN." Where is my father? I squint to see him near the dugout, his hands cupped around his mouth. My brother swings the bat, and the ball sails, sails, sails out of sight. Everyone stands up, cheering, but I stay seated long enough to write: "THE BIG BROTHER JUST MADE A HOME RUN AND I THINK THATS ALL I'LL WRITE. GOOD-BYE." My brother prances around the bases, casual and grown-up and intelligent, slapping the hands held out in high fives as he trots past third.

The catcher already sulks unmasked against the backstop. My brother casu-
ally taps his foot against home.

On that scrap of paper, I naturally turn toward the people in my life as
a way to begin a description of that life. As a child, it's nearly impossible to
think of myself as an individual separate from my family. And already, as
a novice autobiographer, I see myself spurred by the impulses to document
(here is the world, defined by mother, father, brothers), to explore emotion
(oh, the harsh treatment I receive at my brothers' hands!), and to transcribe
events as they occur (a home run!). In a sense, I'll repeat these impulses over
and over throughout the years as I grow into a writer, hopefully refining
them a little bit along the way.

—BRENDA

Situating Yourself in Relation to Family

From the minute we arrive in the world, we're put at the mercy of the people
who care for us. And we might find the rest of our lives taken up with dual,
contradictory impulses: to be an integral part of this clan and to be a separate individual, set apart. Our families, however they're configured, provide
our first mirrors, our first definitions of who we are. And they become our
first objects of love, anger, and loyalty. No wonder so much creative nonfiction is written about family. How can we really get away from these people?
How have they shaped who we are in the world? And how do our particular
families reflect issues common to us all?

The most important strategy for dealing with family is learning how you
can approach the big issues by focusing on the smallest details. It's often
tempting, especially when you're dealing with emotionally charged material,
to try and encompass *everything* into one essay. Such a strategy will leave you,
and your readers, numb and exhausted. Ask the small questions. Who was
the family member to come last to the table? Who kept (and perhaps hid) a
diary? Who had the most distinctive laugh? Sometimes these questions are
the ones that lead to the biggest answers. For example, in "Reading History
to My Mother," Robin Hemley spurs a complex essay about his mother by
focusing in first on her eyeglasses:

My mother owns at least half a dozen glasses, and I know I should have sorted through them all by now (we tried once). . . . On her dresser there are parts of various eyeglasses: maimed glasses, the corpses of eyeglasses, a dark orphaned lens here, a frame there, an empty case, and one case with a pair that's whole. This is the one I grab and take out to my mother who is waiting patiently, always patient these days, or perhaps so unnerved and exhausted that it passes for patience.

In this memoir, Hemley will detail the decline of his mother's physical and mental health as she advances in age, and he chronicles his own ambivalent responses to caring for her. This subject will lead into even bigger ideas about how we read history to one another, how we re-create our histories as part of our love for one another. Rather than approach such things head-on, Hemley wisely turns to the small, physical things first—those eyeglasses—as a way to not only create a convincing scene, but also to plant the seeds for the emotional material to come. Those mangled, mixed-up eyeglasses signal the state of mind we'll be invited to enter.

The Biographer

When we're writing about family, sometimes it's helpful to think of ourselves as biographers, rather than autobiographers. This slight shift in perspective just might be enough to create the emotional distance necessary to begin shaping experience into literature on the page. It will also allow you to take a broader view of your subject that encompasses community, culture, and history. It will still be a *subjective* account—all biographies filter through the mind and emotional perspective of a writer—but it will be an account that has managed to take a wider view.

Sometimes it's helpful to imagine our relatives as they must have been before we knew them as mother, father, grandmother, and so forth. In Paisley Rekdal's essay "The Night My Mother Met Bruce Lee," for example, she allows herself to imagine in vivid detail her mother as a sixteen-year-old girl:

Age sixteen, my mother loads up red tubs of noodles, teacups chipped and white-gray as teeth, rice clumps that glue themselves to the plastic tubs' sides or dissolve and turn papery in the weak tea sloshing around the bottom. She's at Diamond Chan's restaurant, where most of her cousins work after school and during summer vacations some of her friends, too. . . . My mother's nails are cracked, kept short by clipping or gnawing, glisten only when varnished with the grease of someone else's leftovers.

We then move from this imaginative scene into a "real" one closer to the present day; the contrast between the two allows for a kind of understanding and character development that would otherwise be impossible.

If you were to take on the mantle of the biographer, how could you begin to see the members of your family differently? How can you combine the objectivity of a researcher with the subjectivity of the biographer? You'll find that even if you haven't written a full-fledged biography, you will have found fresh ways to conceptualize those people who are closest to you.

The Obstacle Course

When we write about family, we set ourselves up for a plethora of ethical, emotional, and technical issues that may hinder us from writing altogether. It's one thing to write about your sister in your diary; it's quite another to write about her in an essay published in a national magazine. And when we set out to write about family, we are naturally going to feel compelled to break long silences that may have kept the family together in the first place. In recent years, many creative nonfiction works have emerged that take on issues of child abuse, incest, alcoholic parents, and other emotionally charged issues. When you sit down to write, you might feel obligated to write about traumas of your family history. You might feel these are the only issues "worth" tackling in literature.

Family is always an enormous subject, and as writers, we must find a way to handle this subject with both aplomb and discretion. If your family history is particularly charged, it will be even more essential for you to find the smaller details—the miniscule anecdotes—that will lead the way into a successful essay. This is not to say that you can't or won't take on the big issues. But they must arrive on the page less as issues and more as scenes, images, and metaphors that will evoke a strong response from the reader.

Permission to Speak

While drafting your essay, you must instinctively drown out the voices that tell you *not* to write. Your mother, father, sisters, and brothers must all be banished from the room where you sit at your desk and call up potentially painful or embarrassing memories. But once you know you have an essay that is more for public consumption than private venting, you have some difficult decisions to make. How much of this is really your own story to tell?

Writers deal with this dilemma in a variety of ways. Some merely remain in denial, convincing themselves that no one—least of all their families—will ever read their work. Some go to the opposite extreme, confessing to their families about their writing projects and asking permission to divulge certain stories and details, giving them complete veto power. Some, such as Frank McCourt with *Angela's Ashes*, wait until the major players have died so that they can no longer be hurt by the exposure or pass judgment on the writer. Some decide that writing about this material in a nonfiction form is just too risky and decide to present their work as fiction instead. Some writers change the names of their characters—some even go so far as to write under a pseudonym—to protect both themselves and their families.

However you choose to negotiate these tricky issues, remember that your story *is* your story to tell. Yours is not the *only* story or perspective on family or on your community, but it is a perfectly valid voice among the chorus. In her essay "Writing About Family: Is It Worth It?" Mimi Schwartz reminds us that "a memoirist, in particular, must think of truth as having a small 't,' not a big one—as in *my* truth rather than *the* truth." And if you examine this truth with a healthy sense of perspective and with literary skill, you may be surprised at the reactions you evoke among your subjects. They may feel honored to see themselves couched in a work of literature and grateful to discover aspects of you they never realized before.

Here is how Robin Hemley dealt with these issues when he wrote and published "Reading History to My Mother."

I think this is one of the few essays I haven't shown my mother. . . . I don't think that one needs to show everything one writes to those involved—sometimes one can actually do more harm than good with the full-disclosure impulse. Sometimes, one acts more out of one's own need for absolution rather than actually considering the feelings of the person to whom the dis-

closure is made. . . . We write for many different reasons, and often our best work is dangerous, edgy, and guilt-inducing. Sometimes we feel it's worth sharing with others, whether the reasons are literary or therapeutic, and I don't think we should necessarily engage in self-censorship simply because we might be unwilling to share our work with the person(s) the work deals with. . . . I'd say that my decision was made of equal measures of love and cowardice.

Love and *cowardice* might aptly describe all of us when we find ourselves writing about family or about those close to us in our communities. Complex emotions beset us in this endeavor, and we must remain aware of them before they ambush us altogether.

If we are going to write successfully about family, our motives must be more than simple exposure of family history and secrets. We must have some *perspective* on our experience that spurs the essay beyond our own personal "dirty laundry" and into the realm of literature. (See Chapter 8 for a discussion of the dangers of "revenge prose" and "the therapist's couch.")

Our role as writers can be that of the witness. We continually bear witness to those around us, and sometimes our job is to speak for those who have never spoken for themselves. When we write about our families or take on the mantle of the biographer, we are really writing (and forging) community. As Terry Tempest Williams writes, in her essay "A 'Downwinder' in Hiroshima, Japan": "I think about . . . how much we need to hear the truth of one another's lives. . . . The Japanese have a word, *aware*, which speaks to both the beauty and pain of our lives, that sorrow is not a grief one forgets or recovers from but is a burning, searing illumination of love for the delicacy and strength of our relations."

Think of yourself as a witness and your writing will take on greater weight and urgency. As you write about the other people who populate your memories and life, you will do so with a clearer sense of purpose that will elevate your writing beyond the purely personal.

TRY IT

1. Try to reconstruct the names of your matriarchal or patriarchal lineage. For instance, what is the name of your mother, your mother's mother, your mother's mother's mother, and so forth? How far back can you go? For instance, in Brenda's case, she once started an essay with the line, "I am the daughter of Sandra, the daughter of Beatrice, the daughter of Pearl." Naming them brings them to life and enables you to begin writing about them. Where do the names come from? Does your own name have any "inheritance" attached to it? What are the stories behind the names? Are you adopted? How does this affect how you construct your sense of lineage?

> VARIATION: Circle one of the names that intrigues you for whatever reason, then do some research on this person. Find photographs, letters, or birth certificates—whatever might be stored in a family archive. Begin an essay that builds a portrait of this person from the name outward.

2. Describe every member of your family in terms of a part of the body. For instance, describe the hands of your mother, father, siblings, grandparents, and yourself. How are they alike? How are they different? Push this exercise further by going for the smallest images. Look at belly buttons, fingerprints, moles, toenails, or tongues. If necessary, imagine the details. For instance, imagine your grandmother's hands as they were before she was a grandmother. Which traits emerge in your own physical makeup? Which ones do you hate? Which ones do you love? How do you imagine you will look twenty years from now? Forty? Fifty?

3. Begin an essay by imagining the life of someone close to you—a family member, friend, mentor—before you knew them. Use your imagination coupled with your experience of this person. Use any clues that may exist: objects from the past, documents, photographs, and so forth to form a portrait of this person before you were in the picture. Then complete the essay by contrasting this portrait with the person you know today. How are they different or similar?

4. Almost all families have some mythic story about someone meeting a famous person. Try to re-create a relative's encounter with a celebrity.

5. Create a picture of your family based on some simple gesture: the way they sigh, laugh, cry, or kiss. Begin with a vivid, original description of this gesture, then describe your father, your mother, yourself, or any other family members. Try to see how examining these small gestures reveals larger details about the family. (You can track down Bernard Cooper's essay "The Fine Art of Sighing," located in the book *Truth Serum*, as a model if you like.)

6. Write a family story in a voice other than your own. Use the point of view of another family member and see how the story changes or which details now become important.

7. Write a list of the subjects you would "never" write about. What are the silences that can't be broken? Begin each sentence with "I would never write about" or "I am slow to write about." See if this backward maneuver might actually lead you into scenes, details, and memories you *might* be able to handle in a short essay.

3

"Taking Place":
Writing the Physical World

If you live in a place—any place, city or country—long enough and deeply enough you can learn anything, the dynamics and inter-connections that exist in every community, be it plant, human, or animal—you can learn what a writer needs to know.
—GRETEL EHRLICH

I am writing about the first place I remember living, casting around for a way to write about it that fits in with what I've learned is acceptable in the literature of place. Elizabeth, New Jersey: people who know the city shudder and mention the rows of smokestacks craning along the side of the New Jersey Turnpike. I spent my early years there, and along with a rickety shore bungalow, it's the place I have the most visceral childhood attachment to. But when I think of the writing of childhood place I think of Vladimir Nabokov's Speak, Memory, *with the majestic beauty of pre-Revolutionary St. Petersburg; of Annie Dillard's wooded rambles in* An American Childhood. *How do you write about a vacant lot glinting with glass, where I spent many ecstatic hours as a child, a cemetery where my brother and I played? It was as scary and luminous a childhood as any other. Does place matter only when it carries its own transcendent beauty? How do you memorialize the seemingly unbeautiful?*

After many false starts, I begin writing about my early home by reflect-ing on the city's name. "Elizabeth," I write, "had a Queen's name. Every land's an extension of the monarch's body, a great green I Am of the royal person, and Elizabeth's city showed she'd been gone a long time. It was gassy and bad-smelling as any dead woman."

The Elizabeth of the city, I learned much later, was not Queen Eliza-beth, as I'd thought, but some other woman. No matter. It was what I believed at the time of writing, and what I believed, for some reason, as a child. The interest of the place was not in its beauty, its own transcendent qualities, but the way it bounced off my life and the lives of those around me: the character it became.

—SUZANNE

Start Looking

Where are you reading this book? Put it down for a second and look around you; take into account what is both inside and outside the space you're in. In your mind, run over the significance of this place. Are you somewhere that has meaning for you because it is the place you grew up or because it is not? Does this place represent freedom or responsibility? Is it someplace tempo-rary for you or permanent? When you force yourself to look around carefully and openly, do you thrill to the natural beauty or respond to its urban excite-ment? Or are you somewhere now you feel you could never call home?

Our responses to place are some of the most complex we'll ever experience. Our sense of visual beauty, our psychological drive for comfort and familiar-ity in our environment, and our complex responses to loaded concepts such as "nature" and "home" embed place with layers of significance. Although fic-tion writers typically have the importance of location and setting driven into them, it is easy for nonfiction writers to forget that they, too, must be situ-ated physically. We find that an essayist with a wonderful story to tell—a fam-ily story, say, of a troubled Vietnam-vet father or of raising an autistic child—will typically leave out the vital backdrop of the story: a supportive small town, a resource-rich city, or a town in which the family's story unfolds against a background of petty bigotry and misunderstanding.

Where We're Writing From

We, Brenda and Suzanne, landed—through various tracks—in the smallish city of Bellingham, Washington, on the Puget Sound, under a volcano called Mt. Baker that is presently giving off steam from under-earth vents called *fumaroles*. On the one hand, our lives are peaceful. We teach classes, write, attend a film or concert now and then, and work on this book. On the other hand, every few years the mountain issues this fleecy reminder that it has more control than we ever give it credit for. Under its crust is enough molten rock to turn our lives into something else entirely.

Environments tend to function as informing elements that we take for granted and edit out of our stories until they act up. We who live here may notice that people become quieter and more lethargic during our gray, rainy winter months, bursting back into exuberant life when the sun returns. Nevertheless, it takes a certain amount of awareness to relate the way our lives unfold to the fact that we live here, in the maritime Northwest, rather than somewhere else. (And in fact, when the first draft of this chapter was written, we experienced the powerful Nisqually earthquake, centered south of Seattle, which sent our computers dancing and our certainties about the ground beneath our feet shaking along with them.)

Before proceeding any further in this chapter, pull out an essay you've already written and check to see if locations and physical settings are established. Can we hear how a key conversation was heightened by the silence of a forest clearing? Do we see and smell the banyan trees of South Florida rather than the cedars of the Northwest? If you write of a town or a city, is its physical location and socioeconomic character clear?

Setting Scenes: Place as Character

In Chapter 12, "The Basics of Good Writing in Any Form," we discuss in depth the techniques of scene-setting and its importance in nonfiction. It seems useful to touch on that topic here as well. Nonfiction writers use place frequently as a primary subject. Even if you never do, however, the place where a story unfolds plays a vital role. In all the elements of setting a scene—character, dialogue, place, action—place can be the easiest one to overlook.

Would *Jane Eyre* have been the same book without her tale unfolding against the backdrop of Thornfield, that gabled mansion with its nests of crows? Would Huckleberry Finn's adventures have had the same resonance without the silvery roil of the Mississippi River? Your own story needs the same depth of field. One useful way to judge your own scene-setting is to think of place as a character unto itself. In the excerpt from the essay "Elizabeth" at the start of this chapter, the city takes on the character of a woman: an aging, decayed figure against which the children's exploits take on an incongruous irony.

Writing About Home

For nonfiction writers, particularly memoirists, the place of childhood has a critical importance. It is the primal map on which we plot life's movements. It is the setting of the rich mythology that is earliest memory (see Chapter 1), the enchanted forest in which our benighted characters wander, looking for breadcrumbs and clues and facing down their demons. If you draw your earliest place of memory—a bedroom, say, or a favorite hiding place in an apartment or a yard—you will, by the highly selective and emotional process of memory, be drawing an emotional landscape of your childhood.

Maybe you remember the deep, sagging chair that attracted and frightened you because it was sacred to your father and he sank into it in the evening, angry from the day's work. Or perhaps you remember the table where your family sat around and ate kimchi, which none of your friends ate and of which you learned to be vaguely ashamed. Maybe you recall the soft woolly smell of your covers at night or the dim blue glow of a nightlight. This is home, the place where the complex person you are came into being. And understanding the concept of home and its physical character is key to understanding the many different individuals you'll write about in your nonfiction.

When Home Is Away

Bharati Mukherjee, an Indian-American writer, says home to her is a place she has never been and that no longer exists in a national sense. At the time of her father's birth, his village was in India. Now it is part of Bangladesh. As a woman of Indian descent, she defines her home patrilineally, making her a citizen of an unknown place, bearing ethnic claims that no longer make any sense. In her essay "A Four-Hundred-Year-Old Woman," she writes:

> *I was born into a class that did not live in its native language. I was born into a city that feared its future, and trained me for emigration. I attended a school run by Irish nuns, who regarded our walled-off school compound in Calcutta as a corner (forever green and tropical) of England. My "country"—called in Bengali* desh, *and suggesting more a homeland than a nation of which one is a citizen—I have never seen. It is the ancestral home of my father and is now in Bangladesh. Nevertheless, I speak his dialect of Bengali, and think of myself as "belonging" to Faridpur.*

Later, Mukherjee writes that for her, "the all too real Manhattan [her present home] and Faridpur have merged as 'desh.'"

For most Americans, the terms *home* and *native* are probably loaded with connotations we rarely pause to tease out. We—Brenda and Suzanne—for example, celebrate different holidays. We bake our traditional breads—challah and panettone—and mark rites of passage with chopped liver or the dried fish called *baccala* without much awareness of how those foods reflect what was available and affordable in our families' countries of origin, or the poverty and threat reflected in the fact that our not-too-distant forebears came to be here. There are stories in these deeply personal, everyday connections and disconnections in American lives.

Writing About Nature

If we think of place as character, we should add that no "character" comes with as many preconceptions as nature. Drawing energy from early writers like Thoreau, American essayists have always had a particular affinity with nature writing. This country in its present national incarnation is new—the "new country" that creates by being in opposition to the "old country" of the preceding discussion. For much of its life, it has defined itself by its wilderness, by the sense of frontier to be explored and frequently controlled. And even as the American wilderness vanishes, literature faces the question of what we have lost with it, along with the buffalo, sequoia, and deep old-growth forests breathing so recently out of our past.

In his classic memoir *Walden; Or, Life in the Woods*, Henry David Thoreau's declarations become a charge to nature writers and nature seekers for generations to come: "I went to the woods because I wished to live deliberately, to front only the essential facts of life, and see if I could not learn what it had to teach, and not, when I came to die, discover that I had not lived." American literature's historic distrust of civilization (think of *Huckleberry Finn*) has created a particular reverence for nature writing in our country. Writers like Thoreau teach us that recording the experiences of the individual removed from society—one on one with the physical world that created him or her—provides an avenue to "live deep and suck out all the marrow of life."

Thoreau's approach to nature—as a way of paring life down to its essentials, finding oneself—continues in the work of writers such as Wendell Berry. In essays like "An Entrance to the Woods," Berry describes how on a hiking trip, "Today, as always when I am afoot in the woods, I feel the possibility, the reasonableness, the practicability of living in the world in a way that would enlarge rather than diminish the hope of life."

To Berry and Thoreau, nature represents life at its most basic—life at the bone. But in the literary world, few subjects are as complex in their symbolic structure as nature. To Wordsworth, it was the ultimate muse, the "anchor of his purest thoughts." To others, it's simply the ultimate power.

What does nature mean to you? For those with a nature-writing bent, it's deceptively simple to wax rhapsodic about the cathedral beauty of old-growth forests or the piercing melodies of the thrush. In other words, we tend to approach nature writing first and foremost as description. While fine description is dandy, it tends to wear thin after a while. Even if your prose about the soft rosy beauty of the alpenglow is first rate, if you don't move beyond that, readers are likely to want to put your writing down and go see for themselves.

What holds readers in the works of writers like Berry and Thoreau is the sense of a *human consciousness* moving through nature, observing it, reacting to it, and ultimately being transformed by it. Thoreau's description of his cottage at Walden Pond is instructive:

> *I was seated by the shore of a small pond. . . . I was so low in the woods that the opposite shore, half a mile off, like the rest, covered with wood, was*

my most distant horizon. For the first week, whenever I looked out on the pond it impressed me like a tarn high up on the side of a mountain, its bottom far above the surface of other lakes, and, as the sun arose, I saw it throwing off its nightly clothing of mist, and here and there, by degrees, its soft ripples or its smooth reflecting surface was revealed, while the mists, like ghosts, were stealthily withdrawing in every direction into the woods.

Notice how Thoreau embeds his basic concept of living in nature as stripping human life bare in this very description. Not only is it beautifully poetic, but we see Walden Pond looming huge in front of him, throwing off its obscuring mists, as a kind of mirror for Thoreau's consciousness, coming clear in nature and throwing off the layer of fog of human convention.

Remember Scott Russell Sanders's essay "Buckeye" from the "Touch" section of Chapter 1? Later in the essay, Sanders describes how his father, a born naturalist, once stripped the husk from a buckeye to show it to his son. "He picked up one, as fat as a lemon, and peeled away the husk to reveal the shiny seed. He laid it in my palm and closed my fist around it so the seed peeped out from the circle formed by my index finger and thumb." Here, the buckeye seems to come alive, almost hatching from the author's hand. It's an image of the life both men find in nature, as well as an image of the father coming alive in the author's memory.

When you think of your feelings about nature, think about Thoreau and Sanders, and the question of how what you see before you embodies larger forces: an aspect of the human condition or the tenderness and toughness of a person you know. Use that larger element as a way into your essay.

Writing About the Environment

In "An Entrance to the Woods," Wendell Berry goes beyond merely describing the woods or the way in which his hiking and camping experience lends perspective to his own human existence. As a nonfiction writer who is constantly pushing himself to examine with the broadest possible lens what exists at the tips of his fingers (which all good nonfiction writers do), he asks himself how he as a human being embodies the larger interaction of human and nature. It's an interrelationship that's become problematic at the beginning of the twenty-first century, as we face global warming and the last century's out-pouring of industrial pollution.

While in the woods, Berry hears the roar of a car in the distance and writes, "That roar of the highway is the voice of the American economy; it is sound-ing also wherever strip mines are being cut in the steep slopes of Appalachia, and wherever cropland is being destroyed to make roads and suburbs. . . ." It is a wonderful moment in the essay, of opening out and refocusing from a simple, enlightening natural experience to a critique of human intervention in the natural order that we've come to label the *ecosystem*.

Typically, a writer sitting down to compose a nature essay such as Berry's would "erase" that car motor from his or her record of this occasion, simply leave it out; it is tempting in nonfiction to pare down our experiences to those sights and sounds that make a unified whole. A passing mention of the noise as an anomaly—out of tone with the peaceful surroundings—would also be a natural move to make. It would be a far less important and less honest tack, though, than Berry's turn, which was to discuss how these woods in the essay exist in uneasy, threatened relationship to the human-dominated world around them.

Travel Writing

Often, a sense of place comes into sharp focus when we travel off our own turf and into lands foreign to us. Our survival instincts take over, and we grow alert as cats, turning our heads at the call of the *muezzin* in the mosque, sniffing out the smell of roasted lamb in the market stall, spying an old man bearing a homemade wooden coffin up the alleyways of a walled city. In the context of travel, "place" begins to seem not so much the land itself, but every-thing and anything associated with the land: its people, animals, food, music, religion—all the things that make up life itself.

Pico Iyer, a consummate travel writer, sums it up this way: "We travel, ini-tially, to lose ourselves; and we travel, next, to find ourselves. We travel to open our hearts and eyes and learn more about the world than our newspa-pers will accommodate. . . . And we travel, in essence, to become young fools again—to slow time down and get taken in, and fall in love once more."

Your task, as a good travel writer, is to both pay attention to the details of place—in all their glorious particularities, with all their good points and bad—and to render these details in a voice that is wholly your own. You must situate yourself as both participant and observer, always ready for the unexpected, but armed with the many lenses that enable you to interpret this world for your readers in a way they've never heard before.

This mandate requires you to find a purpose for your writing *above and beyond* the travel experience itself. Otherwise, you will produce a piece of writing akin to those slide shows we all dread: the summons into a friend's living room to view her pictures of last summer's vacation. "And here we are at the Louvre," the hostess quips brightly, while her guests nod off behind her on the couch in the flickering light of the slide projector. If you expect the travels themselves to carry the weight of narrative interest, you will end up with an essay that looks disconcertingly like: "First I went here, then I went here, and look what an amazing/horrible/fascinating/soul-searing time I had!" Eventually, no one will care. They will sneak out your living room the back way, leaving you alone with your out-of-focus slides. The places themselves may be intrinsically fascinating, but if you render them into flat landscapes, you'll be left with the lame protest, "Well, you just had to have been there."

In a way, the demands of travel writing can epitomize the challenges of any kind of creative nonfiction writing. How do you shape or draft the work so that the experience becomes *more* than itself? How do you relinquish the role of the transcriber and take on the mantle of the artist? Critic Paul Fussell answers that question this way: "Successful travel writing mediates between two poles: the individual physical things it describes, on the one hand, and the larger theme that it is 'about' on the other. That is, the particular and the universal."

For instance, to come back to Pico Iyer once more, his books not only describe his travels into places as diverse as the L.A. airport, Burmese temples, and suburban Japan, but they also often become inquiries into the effects of globalization on the world's cultures. Born to Indian parents in England, then living for a long time in California, Iyer brings with him his deep-seated—almost innate—awareness of how modern cultural boundaries have begun to blur. He begins his book *Video Night in Kathmandu* with a description of how Sylvester Stallone's movie character Rambo had infiltrated every

cinema in Asia during his visit there in 1985. By using this one specific example as a focus, he sets the tone and purpose for the book. "I went to Asia," he
writes a few pages into the first chapter, "not only to see Asia, but also to see
America, from a different vantage point and with new eyes. I left one kind of
home to find another: to discover what resided in me and where I resided
most fully, and so to better appreciate—in both senses of the word—the
home I had left."

With this kind of sensibility, Iyer gains the trust of the reader. Here we
know we are in the hands of a traveler who has experienced a place not only
as a tourist, but as an intellectual, an artist, and a pilgrim. We can read his
books, yes, to get tips on how to survive those twelve-hour bus trips, or we
can read to enjoy the characters and scenes he re-enacts (his description of
the bicycle trishaw driver in Mandalay will stay with you long after the book
is done). But these details are held within a much greater context. In this way,
he travels with a purpose that allows a sense of place to penetrate him and his
readers on many levels at once.

You will find that good travel writers avoid the pitfalls that lead to self-
serving or clichéd writing. They not only have a heightened perception, a precise attention to language, and a facility with scene-making, but also a marked
generosity innate in the writer's stance, a perception that sees the foibles of the
world and forgives them. In much of the beginning writing we see about
travel, the writer falls into stereotypes about other tourists and the native people; he begins to either make fun of or put down the others he encounters on
his travels. Such a stance not only becomes distasteful to the reader, but it
betrays an insufficient maturity on the part of the writer to understand what
is important and what is not. His attention to place becomes annoyingly
myopic, and he becomes a whiner, complaining about "all those tourists" while
munching on potato chips in line to the Sistine Chapel, his cameras slung
about his neck. He is guilty of just what he is criticizing: the tourist mental-
ity that sees only the surfaces and complains when the place fails to live up
to expectations.

The other pitfall in travel writing is for the voice to become too much like
a guidebook, commenting heavily on the cleanliness of the bathrooms in a
hotel in downtown Istanbul but missing the dawn light on the Blue Mosque.
As Fussell puts it: "Guidebooks are not autobiographical but travel books are,
and if the personality they reveal is too commonplace and un-eccentric, they

will not be very readable." As with any good creative nonfiction, the *self* must be wholly present in the work, a voice that engages us to take this trip along with you, to stand at the windows and gaze out at what you, *and only you*, choose to show us.

Witnesses to Our World

In the last chapter, we discussed the emerging sense of much nonfiction as a literature of *witness*—the sense that, in a world flooded with activity and change and information sources the public growingly distrusts (rightly or wrongly), the individual voice may provide the ultimate record. In the last decades nothing has changed faster than the environment. The world's population has burgeoned, and technology has developed the ability to clear lands, pollute the air, and drive species to extinction in record time. Your life has witnessed the eclipse of hundreds of thousands of species, even if they passed out of this world without your awareness. (The current rate of species extinction is matched only by that of the age of the dinosaur's demise, sixty-five million years ago.) Your life has also seen the destruction of much natural land and its replacement with man-made habitat, even if this fact too only barely crossed your consciousness.

For instance, if you can remember a time when Rhode Island spent winters buried under several feet of snow—now replaced by light snows and rains—you may be a witness to the phenomenon many would call global warming. Or, if you remember catching salmon or chasing frogs as a child— creatures you now see rarely if at all—you have witnessed the severe recent decline of several indigenous creatures. If you *pay attention*—if you notice the small changes that accumulate in the various places you inhabit—you become a witness.

TRY IT

1. Isolate a single room or outdoor place that to you forms the most essential place of childhood. Quickly write down every element of the place you can remember with as much detail as possible. What were the patterns of the things you see? Are they old or new? Which odd details do you remember (e.g., a gargoyle-shaped knot in the wood, a gray rug with a dark stain the shape of Brazil, and so forth)? Now fill in an emotional tone for each detail. Did the wallpaper make you feel safe or frightened? What were your favorite things in this place to look at? Your least favorite? Why? What felt "yours" and what felt other? Assemble these specifics into an essay about the emotional landscape of your childhood, moving about the room, letting your essay function as an emotional "camera."

2. Many of us, like Mukherjee, find our sense of "desh" blends real and distant—maybe unseen—places. Is your family one of the many in this country that embodies a divided sense of home? What does "home" mean to you, your siblings, your parents? Many contemporary American families are very transient now. As one of our students, whose father had been transferred multiple times as she grew up, put it, "home is where there's a room for me to unpack my things." Think about whether there's a single place—a physical location—your family defines as "home," or what you do as you move around to bring the sense of home with you. If you're adopted, your birth family, whether you know them or not, may represent another concept of home. Consider writing an essay in which you unpack the complex layers of meaning in the word *home*, with specific references to all the possibilities.

3. Is there an "old country" in your family profile? How does it affect your family culture, traditions, or modes of interacting? Write about the ways your family's country or countries of origin cause you to see yourself as different from others in your area, perhaps straddling several very different cultures.

4. Examine a piece of your writing and scrutinize place as character. Is your setting a developed character? What kind of character is it: positive, nurturing, menacing, indifferent? Imagine the setting of a scene as a silent character, shaping and adding nuance to the action surrounding it.

VARIATION: Write a biography of a place. Choose a street, a forest, an airport (possibly look at Pico Iyer's essay on the Los Angeles airport, "Where Worlds Collide," for guidance), a shopping center, anyplace that has character to you, whether positive or negative. Write a profile, a "character study," of that environment.

5. Can you articulate what your own vision of nature is? If the outdoors draws you and brings you a special kind of knowledge or contentment, can you put into words what that connection consists of? What would your metaphor be of the human-nature interaction that is, in many ways, the ground of our lives here on earth? Can you think of a time when you went into a natural setting to make a difficult decision, work something out in your mind, or somehow come to feel more "yourself"? What led you to that place? Did it help you in the way you wanted?

Remember, as you articulate your sense of nature in language, that there's nothing else (besides love, perhaps!) that so easily lends itself to cliché. Tranquil brooks, awesome mountains, trilling birds—these are the stuff of hackneyed authors. Make your description fresh, original, and interesting.

VARIATION: Jennifer Price, who wrote an essay titled "A Brief Natural History of the Plastic Pink Flamingo," writes about *urban nature*, the aspects of nature that thrive in cities—nature stores at malls, even stuffed birds on women's hats. Write about nature without pursuing nature in the traditional sense. Stay in your apartment building or go to a shopping mall and observe the trees, the crow colonies, even the microclimates created by human development.

6. In this era of accelerating change, we ask you to think of your life as a piece of living history. Looking at your life as an intersection of personal history and the environment that surrounds you, to what can you bear witness? Write for about ten minutes, associating freely and spontaneously, about a place of your childhood, a place that for you defines your childhood—the porch of your house, a creek, the fire escape of an apartment, a special place in the woods. What did the place smell, taste, feel like? Include, but don't limit yourself to, the natural elements: air quality and odor, trees, wildlife (including insects).

Now write for ten minutes on what this place is like now, whether from your own current experiences of it or from what you've been told. How has it changed? What is gone now that was there before? What is there now that wasn't there before? Think of yourself as a living history of this place—what changes did you find between the place of your childhood and the place of your adulthood? Do these changes reflect any changes in your own life?

As you compare these two quick writings, see what larger elements emerge. Have you and the place of your childhood changed in tandem or gone in different directions? Are you witness to changes that reflect larger—perhaps dangerous—currents of change in our contemporary world? Think about it: even seemingly small things, like the loss of much of our amphibian life, such as frogs, will alter over time the nature of the planet we live on. Think about your writings in the largest possible sense: often this short exercise unlocks a valuable essay.

7. If you have a travel diary or journal, go back to it now and pull out sections that give highly sensory descriptions of place: the feel of the air, the taste of the food, the sounds, the smells. Type these out in separate sections, then arrange them on a table, seeing if you can find a common theme that may bind an essay together. What can you construe as the greater purpose for your travels? How can you incorporate that purpose into your travel writing? What is the one image that will emerge for metaphorical significance?

8. Take a day to travel your hometown as a tourist. Pretend you've never seen this place before and wander with all your senses heightened. Take a notebook with you and write down your impressions. How can you make the familiar new again?

VARIATION FOR A GROUP: As a group, take this trip together. Then compare notes and see how different eyes perceive different things. Take some time at the end of the day, or a few days later, to write together and see where these sensory impressions might lead.

4

Writing the Spiritual Autobiography

Be patient toward all that is unsolved in your heart and try to love
the questions themselves like locked rooms or like books written in a
very foreign tongue. Do not now seek the answers, which cannot be
given you because you would not be able to live them. . . . Live the
questions now. Perhaps you will then gradually, without noticing it,
live along some distant day into the answer.
                                              —RAINER MARIA RILKE

*Before I sit down at my desk, I look out my window and notice the light as
it reflects off the bay. I light a candle and a stick of incense, reaching over
the small statue of a Buddha sitting on the windowsill. On a shelf above
my desk sits a menorah my parents gave me for Hanukkah one year. A St.
Christopher medal lies coiled in a small compartment in a drawer of my
desk. Photographs of my four great-grandmothers bear witness to all this
spiritual paraphernalia, gazing down at me with what I interpret as amused
benevolence.*

*All of these things— the light off the bay, the incense, the meditating
Buddha, the menorah, St. Christopher, my ancestors—create an atmosphere
of eclectic spirituality that has come to inform much of my writing. From
the very beginning, my writing has tended to chronicle the sometimes baf-
fling turns my spiritual path has taken: from acting as the earnest president
of my Jewish youth group, to drifting through days of Grateful Dead con-
certs in the eighties (convinced of the divinity of Jerry Garcia), to back-
packing solo in the meadows around Mt. Rainier, to meditating in silence
for weeks at a time in California farmhouses. I've settled down a bit in my*

staid middle age, but I've never lost that sense of spiritual quest driving the trajectory of my life.

Now, writing itself seems to be the deepest spiritual act I can perform. So I sit down at my desk. I light my incense. I look out my window and take a deep breath. I feel the presence of my great-grandmothers cheering me on. I write one word and then another. Who knows where it will lead? What kind of faith can I muster to continue? I don't know. It's a little like prayer, a little like meditation, a little like walking an unknown trail in the high country.

—BRENDA

The Tradition of Spiritual Autobiography

Though oftentimes invisible in our lives, spirituality seems to follow us everywhere. From the moment we're born, we're initiated into a world that relies on many different rituals to guide us. Or, if we're born into a family more secular, we become aware of ourselves in opposition to predominant modes of religious belief. Perhaps that is why we've lately noticed a renaissance in memoirs that use either religion or spirituality as a guiding narrative or metaphor.

But the impulse to write spiritual autobiography has been around as long as human consciousness. The form keeps adapting to fit whatever culture and society demand of it. These works range from devotional narratives to science writing that finds spiritual fodder in the cells of the human body, but the basic structure usually wins out. These narratives tend to focus on moments of insight that lead the narrator in a new direction. By their very nature, many spiritual autobiographies appear to mimic or echo classic "conversion" stories found in religious texts: the protagonist is lost and then found, and the narratives hinge on precise moments of "turning," either away or toward points of reference identified as God, Allah, Yahweh, the Great Spirit, and so on.

These conversions may also work the opposite way, especially after defining events such as the Holocaust or the terrorist attacks of September 11, 2001. The narrator moves from a place of religious or spiritual certainty to one that is more fragmented or full of doubt.

We can call these moments "epiphanies" (sudden insights), but they don't necessarily arrive with the bang the term suggests. They may be quiet moments, barely noticeable until the act of writing magnifies their significance. A turning point can be as subtle as Emily Dickinson's "certain slant of light" into a room, or Virginia Woolf's contemplation of a dying moth in her study.

The Quest Narrative

Full-length spiritual autobiographies essentially take the form of a *quest narrative*, propelled by burning questions, a journey toward an unclear destination. The protagonist sets herself on a path, encounters obstacles and unexpected guides, and is transformed along the way. For example, *The Wizard of Oz* could be the most traditional and metaphoric of spiritual autobiographies. The protagonist, Dorothy, driven by deep, inchoate longing, finds herself on a journey in an unknown country. Essentially alone, she must rely on guidance from unexpected sources to find her way toward a vague, promised land. She encounters many obstacles along the way, many turning points, but finally arrives at Oz, only to find the destination nothing like what she imagines. When she finally returns home, she is the same person but transformed by her quest.

Spirituality does not necessarily need to be contained in religions or places of worship. Nature writer John Muir, rather than turning away or toward an external spiritual figure or destination, includes spirituality in all of nature. In *My First Summer in the Sierra*, Muir writes, "In our best times everything turns into religion, all the world seems a church and the mountains altars." *How interesting everything is*, he muses throughout the book, a good mantra any writer can take to heart.

Personal Renditions of the Sacred

As with any strong work of creative nonfiction, the successful spiritual autobiography hinges on discovery through the writing process itself. The writer does not set out to give us predetermined answers but instead allows us some insight into the questions that drive him. Spiritual autobiographies, in particular, "find interesting" the turns in the road and the roadside attractions; they do not necessarily follow a straight line but proceed more intuitively, meandering from point to point in a way that may seem digressive, but actually forms a clear path in retrospect.

In *Traveling Mercies*, Anne Lamott's wry account of her own spiritual process, she puts it this way:

> *My coming to faith did not start with a leap but rather a series of staggers from what seemed like one safe place to another. Like lily pads, round and green, these places summoned and then held me up while I grew. . . . When I look back on some of these early resting places—the boisterous home of the Catholics, the soft armchair of the Christian Science mom, adoption by ardent Jews—I can see how flimsy and indirect a path they made. Yet each step brought me closer to the verdant pad of faith on which I somehow stay afloat today.*

If you look on your life as a series of "lily pads," the way Anne Lamott does, you may be able to begin an essay structured around these turning points in your spiritual narrative.

Once you set out to examine your own spiritual inclinations, you will find yourself with a new set of writing dilemmas. Spirituality can be an arena fraught with prefabricated rhetoric and tired clichés. As a writer, your challenge is to find a language and a form so personal that *only you* can give us this rendition of the spiritual life. You must remain aware of how your brand of spirituality has been depicted in the past and find a way to circumvent your reader's expectations and resistance. How do you even begin to discuss spirituality without immediately using language that has lost its meaning from overuse?

As we saw in the last three chapters, powerful writing always emerges from the physical, specific, and sensory details of your experience. If you decide to write about spiritual experience—whether positive or negative—you will want to look closely at the physical elements that make up your spiritual life, whether those include incense in a church, chanting in a synagogue, or the odor of cedar on your daily walk. Beginning there, ask yourself how your sense of spirituality informs your life and the lives of those around you.

You could also approach your spiritual autobiography by becoming a "layperson's expert." Poet Kathleen Norris, author of *The Cloister Walk* and other books on faith, creates a lyrical yet highly researched version of spirituality when she immerses herself in the world of a Benedictine monastery. In *Virgin Time*, Patricia Hampl makes a pilgrimage to the roots of her spirituality and presents a "travelogue" of faith that includes not only her own experience but a great deal of "expert" information.

In contrast to Norris and Hampl, who become friendly experts and guides, Anne Lamott takes on the role of the endearing screwup, a woman who tries her best, often falling short but able to recover. She becomes more of a buddy to the reader, articulating all those weaknesses we thought must be kept hidden. Lamott maintains a sense of irony throughout her writings on faith, a conversational voice that trusts the reader as much as we grow to trust her. One pitfall of spiritual writing is that it can become too heavy and self-absorbed; Lamott provides a good model for an alternative voice, one that claims no perfection in the spiritual life.

What Is Your "Koan?"

In his essay "The Mickey Mantle Koan," memoirist and novelist David James Duncan sets himself a koan, a puzzle or riddle given to Zen students by their masters, the answer to which might lead to spiritual enlightenment. In Duncan's case, the koan takes the form of a signed baseball sent to his dying brother by Mickey Mantle. The brother dies before the baseball arrives, and for more than twenty years it sits on Duncan's shelf—intriguing, puzzling, infuriating. Duncan knows the ball offers some clue to sorting out his grief about his brother's death, but he doesn't really know *how* it will do so.

In the essay, Duncan pushes at this "koan" and works it out before our eyes. He takes a simple, almost mundane object—a signed baseball—and gazes at it until it yields some answers. He approaches spirituality not on the level of the abstract but on a grassy playing field, where dirty old balls "hiss and pop" into the gloves of teenage boys:

From the moment I'd first laid eyes on it, all I'd wanted was to take that immaculate ball out to our corridor on an evening just like this one, to take my place near the apples in the north and find my brother waiting beneath the immense firs to the south. All I'd wanted was to pluck that too-perfect ball off its pedestal and proceed, without speaking, to play catch so long and hard that the grass stains and nicks and the sweat of our palms would finally obliterate every last trace of Mantle's blue ink, till all he would have sent us was a grass-green, earth-brown, beat-up old baseball. Beat-up old balls were all we'd ever had anyhow. They were all we ever needed.

When you set about to write your personal rendition of spirituality, look for the concrete *things* of the world that will help you find your own koan. What are the essential questions these objects trigger in you? These questions will help you move, as a writer, from the abstract to the concrete.

Above all, maintain *honesty*—with yourself and your reader. If it has been said before, don't say it. If you veer into platitude and cliché, veer right out of it again. If you find yourself mired in complaint, laugh your way out of it. Render the spiritual life with the same intuition and intelligence you bring to all your work. Find the details, the tone, the rhythms that will separate your voice from the choir's. Sing a solo. Be brave. Really belt it out.

Writing as a Spiritual Practice

Writing is the only way I know how to pray.
—HELENA MARIA VIRAMONTES

Often writers find that the writing process itself grows akin to spiritual practice. It requires the same kind of patience, ritual, and faith. In her book *The Writing Life*, Annie Dillard compares writing to sitting at a desk thirty feet off the ground. "Your work," she writes, "is to keep cranking the flywheel that turns the gears that spin the belt in the engine of belief that keeps you and your desk in midair." Poet Carolyn Forché has called the writer's stance one of "meditative expectancy." Natalie Goldberg, author of *Writing Down the Bones* and *Wild Mind: Living the Writer's Life*, sees writing as an integral part of her Zen practice: "Jack Kornfield, a Vipassana meditation teacher, said last week up at Lama, 'you meditate by yourself, but not for yourself. You meditate for everyone.' This is how we should write."

When we begin to see our writing in this kind of context, we can more easily maintain the patience and faith necessary for our work to be done. It's a secular practice, available to anyone who feels compelled to put pen to paper. When you write this way, you are "living the questions now" and offering up possible pathways into the ineffable.

TRY IT

1. Describe a religious or semireligious ritual that took place in your childhood with some regularity. Use quotes from this ritual as a frame within which you can describe memory, conflict, pleasure, and pain. Move your reader through this ritual with you. Using present tense and vivid imagery, show the emotion you felt about this particular rite as a child.

   VARIATION: Rewrite the scene in the past tense, from an adult perspective. How does your attitude toward this rite change?

2. Try to remember a moment in your childhood when you were first aware of a spiritual presence in your life. This can be anything from a moment within your spiritual tradition, a moment in nature, or a moment when you were alone in your room. Describe this experience from the child's point of view, in the present tense.

   VARIATION: Describe a moment when you were aware of the *absence* of a spiritual presence in your life. Where do these different moments lead you?

3. Put on a piece of music that has spiritual connotations for you: Gregorian chants, bamboo flutes, a Verdi opera, whatever puts you in a meditative mood. Write to this music without ever mentioning it at all.

   VARIATION FOR A GROUP: Each person brings in a piece of music; do the above, with as many pieces as you can in a writing session.

4. If you have a repeating spiritual ritual, give us one particular *scene* out of this rite. Focus on one day, one morning, or one hour that encapsulates what this ritual means to you. Try not to *tell* us what it means, but show us through the details you choose and the tone you create.

5. Imagine yourself into the mind of one of your spiritual ancestors. Which scene or image provides a turning point in your spiritual life even before you're born?

6. Do some research into your spiritual tradition. What are the controversies? How is it practiced in different parts of the world? Interview an elder, or participate in an intensive retreat. Write as both an observer and a participant.

7. Think about the koans that exist in your own life. Which objects, people, places, or situations have always puzzled you? How do these things represent emotions or ideas that you haven't yet been able to articulate? Begin an essay whose goal is to "push" at these objects until they yield some unexpected answers.

8. For the duration of one or two writing sessions, ban certain words from your vocabulary that already have spiritual connotations (*God, Lord, Allah, soul, heart,* scriptural language, and so forth). Often this kind of language becomes a crutch, enabling us to avoid going deeper into our material. Make a list of these words to keep with you. See what moves you have to make to avoid using these words. Which images or scenes arise to take their place?

> **VARIATION FOR A GROUP:** Make a group list of such words and promise to abide by the prohibition for whatever duration the group decides. When reading each other's work, make note of when such words arise and their effect.

5

Gathering the Threads of History

Everyone has his own story, and everyone could arouse interest in the romance of his life if he but comprehended it.
—George Sand

History is nothing more than a thin thread of what is remembered stretched out over an ocean of what has been forgotten.
—Milan Kundera

I am working on a short essay about a strange summer I had when my brother worked for the New Jersey Department of Environmental Protection, running tests on water samples that had been held up for years. He drives a tiny, two-seater Fiat Spider, the car of choice that year. My start: "It's my brother's Spider summer. Not dog days but spider days. My brother has a blue Fiat Spider. It has no backseat but I ride in the back anyway, rolled up in the ten inches or so under the rear window. Spiders aren't much more than human-sized tins so this is risky but it doesn't matter. Let me be a bottle rocket."

What follows is the revised beginning, after a quick search on major events of the year (1974) and surrounding years. I did this search primarily on the Internet, on Historycentral.com's "this year in history" service: "It's my brother's Spider summer. Not dog days but spider days. It's 1974 and things have been crashing. Nixon's resigned or is going to and a few years ago Apollo 13 crash-landed when an oxygen tank blew. (Astronauts in there like Spam in a can, Chuck Yeager said.) Karen Silkwood's about to crash.

My brother has a blue Fiat Spider. It has no backseat but I ride in the back anyway, rolled up in the ten inches or so under the rear window. Spiders aren't much more than human-sized tins so this is risky but it doesn't matter. I am a lost person. Let me be a bottle rocket."

When I add these historical details—the space program, the death of Karen Silkwood—my story becomes enriched and begins to expand outward: connections move back and forth, between the closeness of the car and of space capsules, the sense of questing and uncovering and yet danger that marked that time. The reference to Karen Silkwood adds a reference to those who ask difficult questions, particularly environmental ones, as this book goes on to do. The imminent resignation of President Nixon captures the sense of chaos and rebellion, embodied in these teenagers, so prevalent in our country at that time.

—SUZANNE

Our Historical, Universal Selves

As the preceding experience shows, each of us exists in both a private and a public way. We're all at once son or daughter, lover, sister, brother, neighbor—the person who must have chocolate cereal in the morning and who absently puts the milky bowl down for the cat to lick. We're also pieces of history. We are the people who witnessed the turn of the millennium; we're the first wave of the world's citizens to see their lives transferred more and more onto computer chips. We are also the people who saw the Berlin Wall dismantled, experienced the Monica Lewinsky scandal, and lived through the tragedy of September 11, 2001.

To look at what it means to exist and be human—and who we are as a species—we must look at history. That historical frame is one that may simply enrich your story. Or—as the Kundera quote shows—writing creative nonfiction focused on history might have a deep ethical implication. Sometimes using our own experience of history is a way of preventing that destructive forgetfulness that Kundera describes. Leslie Brody sums up her reasons for writing her book *Red Star Sister*, a memoir of her anti–Vietnam War activism, when she simply said, "You have a responsibility to tell history because people forget history."

The Moose at the Window

Bruce Beasley, a Pacific Northwest writer who teaches nonfiction, is having a conference with a young writer who says she has nothing to write about. The subject for this essay assignment is encountering the natural world. She claims to be utterly without experiences to use.

"We live surrounded by water and mountains," he tells her.

She insists that she likes to stay in, does not hike or camp, and has no feeling for the outdoors.

They go back and forth like this for a while, with Bruce asking question after question about her hobbies, her reaction to her alpine landscape. All are returned with a slightly desperate wail that the subject of nature contains nothing at all she can write about.

"There must be something," he says finally.

"Well," she says hesitantly, "there *was* that moose at the window."

A lost moose had wandered into this northwestern town, and moseyed about for several weeks, making it almost as far as the highway, before being removed by animal control. One morning, this writer woke up and found him—confused, curious, and hungry—staring in the window of her new apartment. The fascinating aspect of nature in her life turned out to be that it had found her—driven by the historical facts of rapid development and loss of habitat. Thinking about this moment as her subject led to a vivid and colorful essay.

Each of us needs to learn to recognize our moose at the window. We've all experienced meeting someone who claimed to be ordinary while finally slipping into the conversation that he or she had grown up on a commune, sung opera as a child, or—like one person we remember—come of age living inside the Statue of Liberty with his Park Service father. The world he grew into, literally seen through the eyes of the Statue of Liberty, is not the same world the rest of us know.

It's important for you as a writer, particularly a nonfiction writer, to think through what is different and important in your world, and what historical events formed the canvas for the fine brushstrokes of your own life. You can easily check the highlights of particular dates and years by using resources like Historycentral.com on the Web or reference books such as *The New York Times Book of Chronologies*.

The "When" in Addition to the "What"

Here is the opening of James Baldwin's famous essay about racism and family, "Notes of a Native Son":

> *On the twenty-ninth of July, in 1943, my father died. On the same day, a few hours later, his last child was born. Over a month before this, while all our energies were concentrated in waiting for these events, there had been, in Detroit, one of the bloodiest race riots of the century. . . . On the morning of the third of August, we drove my father to the graveyard through a wilderness of smashed plate glass.*

Notice that the author's attention operates like a moving camera, panning between familial and national tragedy. Family events come first; then, as if his gaze is forced away, Baldwin takes in the larger chaos of the country's rioting. Right at the start of the essay Baldwin carefully states the season and the year; it's a hot summer month during World War II. Part of the race frustration building up to the riots described here arose from black GIs risking their lives overseas and coming home to face the same old racism, a fact that would have been clear to Baldwin's contemporary audience. By the end of the paragraph, the rioters' smashed glass has become a "wilderness," as if that landscape equals the natural landscape about to close over Baldwin's father's body. The essay accomplishes an unforgettable weaving of personal tragedy with the period that spawned it.

Always keep in mind the extent to which history is the individual writ large, and the individual life is history writ small. Understanding what shapes how you perceive the world—and how you are perceived—is critical to using your own experiences to create strong nonfiction.

TRY IT

You will likely be the last person to recognize what's fascinating—and deeply significant—about you. Your friends will see it, and if you're lucky your family will too. If you're normal, you will brush off their interest, tell them it really wasn't so different—you just don't see what all the fuss is about that last night on board the *Titanic*.

Here's a tool to help you along: a checklist to start yourself off with, whether you choose to answer on paper, in a journal, or in the privacy of your own head. This checklist is designed to elicit a greater awareness of the historical events that have shaped your life, and also a greater awareness of your *social self*—you as conservative or liberal, member of a disadvantaged group, Buddhist, activist, Rosicrucian. While considering these questions, it's important to remember that this social self *always* functions in a cultural and historical context.

1. Many Americans born in the 1950s have powerful early memories of the day President John F. Kennedy was shot—young teachers crying in the classroom, the crackling of televisions left on throughout the day. More recently, most of us vividly remember the events of September 11, 2001. Which event of national or world importance do you remember most clearly? How did you hear of it, and what did you hear? What were other people around you doing? What was going on in your own life that this event bounced off of, resonated with, or formed a strange contrast to? Use all of your senses to re-create this memory.

2. Which aspects of your life do people around you consistently find most interesting? What questions do they ask you? What can you tell them that satisfies/dissatisfies them?

3. At a writer's conference, Leslie Brody talked about living through an unpleasant divorce while the royal wedding of Diana Spencer to the Prince of Wales dominated the news. She talked of the ironies of seeing the two events juxtaposed, and how the memories came to intertuse: the painful sundering of a marriage, the artificial romance of the royal wedding. Which news events formed a backdrop to the most emotional moments of your life? How do the two stories intersect?

4. Try to imagine your own life as someone five hundred years from now might view it. What about your life—the place you live in and the historical unfoldings you've witnessed—do you believe that person would find most interesting? (Hint: what do you find most interesting about life in the past?) How are you a privileged observer?

5. Get in the habit of thinking of yourself in the third person—seeing yourself move through the world as a protagonist—at least once a day. Narrate your daily story to yourself in the third person. As an objective listener (and, to some extent, you can be one), what interests you?

Dating a Significant Event

This is the exercise that helped Suzanne expand her description of the summer of 1974.

1. For the first part, write a description of several paragraphs about a scene or event you consider critical in your life. It should date from at least a few years in your past and can be from childhood. As in most writing exercises, write quickly and do not censor yourself. Be as specific and detailed as possible, using all your senses.

2. Now use a list of chronologies, possibly a simple one printed from an Internet site such as Historycentral.com, to date your experience with a corresponding national or world event. Don't worry if you feel you weren't thinking about the event at the time; your obliviousness to it may be part of what makes the essay fascinating.

3. Once you find a historical corollary, write as many connections, real or metaphoric, as you can. (Suzanne might have written "secrets, cover-ups, crashing, underground corruption, apathy.") In an essay, draw together the two links to show how a critical moment in your life unfolded against a corresponding moment in history. Don't feel the need to justify to yourself immediately why something feels important. If your gut tells you it's important, then surely it is.

6

Writing the Arts

Culture is like a magnetic field, a patterned energy shaping history. It is invisible, even unsuspected, until a receiver sensitive enough to pick up its messages can give it a voice.

—GUY DAVENPORT

I've put up a new picture, a photograph bought for me at an Edward Weston exhibit last April. The composition shows a young woman, all in black, posed against a high, white fence. She half turns toward the camera; her right hand lies tentatively across her heart. The shadow of a leafless tree (I imagine it to be a young oak) curves up and over this slight figure. Actually, it does more than curve; the shadow arches behind her in a gesture of protection. Almost a bow of respect.

Why do I like this picture so much? I glance at it every day, and every day it puzzles me. What draws me to those dark, shaded eyes? What holds me transfixed by the movement of gray shadows over the straight white planks, the drape of the black coat, the white hand raised to the breast in a stunned gesture of surprise?

These questions led me to write the first essay I ever published, titled "Prologue to a Sad Spring," after Weston's own title of the photograph I describe. In this essay, the photograph's mysterious title becomes a meditation on what it means to have a "sad spring," on how our lives are full of losses never memorialized in photographs. It's a short essay, with a circular design that leads the reader back to the appeal of black-and-white photography and to this particular photograph that started the rumination in the first place. Though it's a simple piece, with simple ambitions, it remains a favorite essay in my repertoire. It feels almost like a gift, an ephemeral con-nection between myself and the woman in this photograph, a distant com-muniqué between a writer and a photographer who would never meet.

—BRENDA

The Visual Arts

With old glass-plate daguerreotypes—the earliest form of photography—if you tilt the plate just slightly, the image disappears and the photograph becomes a mirror, an apt metaphor for how the creative nonfiction writer can approach art. Through a close observation of particular paintings, sculptures, or photographs, you can reveal your own take on the world or find metaphors in line with your obsessions. At the same time, you will elucidate that artwork in such a way that the piece will forever after have a greater significance for your reader.

For example, in the essay "Inventing Peace," art historian and journalist Lawrence Weschler closely analyzes a Vermeer painting to understand what is happening during the Bosnian war crimes tribunal in The Hague. He com-pares the serene, almost dreamlike settings of Vermeer with the atrocities the judges in The Hague, just minutes from the Vermeer exhibit, hear about every day. One particular painting, *The Head of a Young Girl*, intrigues him. He explicates this painting for us:

*Has the girl just turned toward us or is she just about to turn away? . . .
The answer is that she's actually doing both. This is a woman who has just
turned toward us and is already about to look away: and the melancholy of
the moment, with its impending sense of loss, is transferred from her eyes to
the tearlike pearl dangling from her ear. . . . The girl's lips are parted in a
sudden intake of breath—much, we suddenly notice, as are our own as we
gaze back upon her.*

Weschler closely studies this painting, interpreting the details as he unfolds them for us one by one. He creates a *speculative narrative* that brings this painting to life. In a speculative narrative, the writer infuses a painting or any situation with a story that arises both from fact and imagination. For instance, it is clear in Weschler's description that the *facts* of the painting exist as he relates them—the parted lips, the pearl earring—but he allows himself to speculate on the *meaning* of those details. He brings his own frame of mind to bear on the portrait; this interpretation sets up the themes for his piece.

Throughout the essay he brings in other voices—art historians, the judges at The Hague, other art patrons, journalists covering the tribunal—until we have a view of Vermeer, and this painting in particular, shaped by Weschler's sensibility and by the context in which he chooses to place the painter. In the end, the image of the girl turning away mirrors an image of one of the war criminals, Dusko Tadic, looking up at a television camera, and then turning away. Both images come to be about loss and the ravages of history:

> *Inventing peace: I found myself thinking of Vermeer with his camera obscura—an empty box fronted by a lens through which the chaos of the world might be drawn in and tamed back to a kind of sublime order.*

As you can see, though the topic is external to the self, Weschler does not sacrifice personal voice. To the contrary, the "I" remains a guiding force throughout the essay: ruminating, reflecting, and questioning his own fascination.

It's important to remember that while nonfiction work about painting is flourishing right now—such as Terry Tempest Williams's *Leap* or Mark Doty's *Still Life with Oysters and Lemon*—photography, sculpture, and installations are all rich subjects for your writing as well. As Tolstoy wrote, art is a language that communicates "soul to soul," on a level that bypasses the intellect. As a writer turning your gaze to the rich, metaphorical world of art, you enter into this dialogue and add to our understanding of the world and ourselves.

The Moving Image Arts

The term *arts* also refers to the moving image arts—television, film, video. A vital and probably the most visible part of our cultural expression, the moving image arts have been somewhat underrepresented in nonfiction and are due for more serious reflection. Remember that although you can find plenty of top-quality film and TV, the art itself doesn't have to be great to warrant your attention. In a brilliant essay titled "Upon Leaving the Movie Theater," Roland Barthes simply writes about the experience of cinema—the darkness of the theater, the unfolding of a narrative in a giant lighted square—as a way of exploring pleasure and our fascination with images.

Remember Paisley Rekdal's "The Night My Mother Met Bruce Lee," from Chapter 2? The essay invokes pop culture images of the Chinese and the Chinese-American, particularly the narrator's mother, whose school guidance counselor advises her not to go to Smith, "hinting at some limitation my mother would prefer to ignore." At the same time, a cook in the restaurant where the mother works tells her he comes from Hong Kong and hence is "*real* Chinese." Rekdal embeds that sense of cultural limbo—appearing Chinese to a white guidance counselor but an assimilated American to a recent immigrant—in the artifice of kung fu movies. In the essay, mother and daughter bond watching the martial arts film *Enter the Dragon*:

> *Bruce Lee narrows his eyes, ripples his chest muscles under his white turtleneck.*
>
> *"I knew him," my mother tells me. "I worked with him in a restaurant when I was in high school."*
>
> *"Really?" This is now officially the only cool thing about her. "What was he like?"*
>
> *"I don't remember. No one liked him, though. All that kung fu stuff; it looked ridiculous. Like a parody."*

Rekdal pays close attention to the film itself in this piece; her prose follows the film's use of lighting—the way Lee's chest "seemed outlined in silver," mirroring the way Rekdal's mother's face "twists into something I do not recognize in the television light." It's as if the cultural distortion created by the movie and movies like it distorts the mother even in the eyes of her daughter. Note that Rekdal has been careful to look at the techniques of the films in question and use them throughout her essay—not just the kung fu itself, which becomes picked up by the restaurant chef, but kung fu films' visual style of bright color and exaggerated gesture.

Films can comment on our own lives and on the history surrounding them. And film and television can capture a cultural moment. Think of how at times movies such as *Thelma and Louise* or TV shows such as "Seinfeld" seem to speak for the feelings of large numbers of people in our society, generating catchphrases and images that become embedded in our collective consciousness. These arts define us personally as well, as Rekdal shows.

As you draft an essay using the moving image arts, think of how you can use those artistic techniques for your own purposes. Can you borrow the visual style of the work in question? Can you write an essay in which you model on scenes in the work you've viewed?

You can also take a more analytical approach to television and film, exploring what they mean in terms of culture and society. For example, Bill McKibben, in his book *The Age of Missing Information*, performs an experiment in which he has friends record every channel on a Virginia cable network for twenty-four hours, then he goes about analyzing what he sees to create a portrait of the American mind-set: what we learn—and, more importantly, what we *don't* learn—from what surrounds us on TV. McKibben, who doesn't own a television himself, spends several months watching these videotapes of a single day's television programming:

> *I began spending eight or ten hour days in front of the VCR—I watched it all, more or less. A few programs repeat endlessly, with half-hour "infomercials" for DiDi 7 spot remover and Liquid Luster car wax leading the list at more than a dozen appearances apiece. Having decided that once or twice was enough to mine their meanings, I would fast-forward through them, though I always slowed down to enjoy the part where the car-wax guy sets fire to the hood of his car.*

As you can see, even though McKibben has set himself a huge, intellectual task, he does not sacrifice his personal voice or his sense of humor to do it. He contrasts what one can learn from a day of television to what one can learn from a day in the woods, providing highly specific examples of each mode, and revealing his own personality at the same time. He turns his attention and powers of observation on something as common as television and enables us to perceive its greater meaning.

Music

As we mentioned in Chapter 1, music can key us into powerful memories that define the self. And music can also serve as a medium to channel some of the most vital issues of our time. We still look back at the 1960s antiwar movement by looking at the music that sprang out of it (and what 1960s documentary would be complete without footage of Country Joe and the Fish's "I Feel Like I'm Fixin' to Die Rag"?). Music is a vessel that holds the emotions of its time.

As an example, let's consider David Margolick, Hilton Als, and Ellis Marsalis's book *Strange Fruit: The Biography of a Song*. "Strange Fruit," a song written for blues singer Billie Holiday, tells the horrendous story of Southern lynchings. Through the lens of this song Margolick, Als, and Marsalis weave together the tales of Holiday's short, heroin-addicted life: the white communist sympathizer who wrote the song, the struggle for civil rights, New York café society, even the history of lynching. This single song contains within it a story that branches out and out to speak of two extraordinary human beings as well as the thorniest problem in American history—race.

Another approach might be to mine your obsession with a particular musician or type of music. For example, in his book *But Beautiful*, Geoff Dyer creates improvisational portraits of eight jazz musicians, getting into their heads, using their points of view. His language and prose style take their cue from jazz, running riffs and hitting discordant notes, as he tries to capture the essence of these musicians on paper. As he explains in the introduction: "When I began writing this book I was unsure of the form it should take. This was a great advantage since it meant I had to improvise and so, from the start, the writing was animated by the defining characteristic of its subject." He calls his book "imaginative criticism," and he uses fictional elements along with the facts of these musicians' lives. The result is a speculative narrative, one that roots itself in music and sings itself on the page.

Literature: The "Reading Narrative"

A fascinating new subgenre of nonfiction has flourished in the last few years— we've titled these works "reading narratives." These essays show the author in different ways reading another piece of literature and using it as a springboard for his or her own actions and reflections. Like writers who use the visual arts, authors of reading narratives are somehow grappling with another artist's aesthetics as a means of probing deeper into their own. Though reading narratives sound simple, they aren't; in good hands, they present a beautifully counterpointed music of two different lives, aesthetics, and meanings. Phyllis Rose's book *The Year of Reading Proust* is an excellent example, as the author reads all of Proust's *Remembrance of Things Past* while using it as a means to chronicle her own life, comparing her Key West to Proust's Balbec, the characters inhabiting her life to those in his.

Most of us can remember at least one "eureka" reading moment. That moment may give us permission to do things differently in our own work: use a new voice, dig deeper, or consider new subject matter as potentially ours. These "eureka" writers are our literary mentors, whether we realize that or not. And what we read may spur us on in many different ways—other authors inspire us, give us permission, and also irritate us in ways that stimulate us to try something new. You can try writing a "literary history" of yourself, one that tracks your life through the many different books you've read and loved.

TRY IT

1. Begin an essay by describing a piece of art that has always intrigued you. Feel free to interpret the details, creating a speculative narrative about what is happening in the painting or what was going through the painter's mind. Find other interpretations from art scholars and begin to create an essay that approaches this artwork from several different angles.

2. Write an essay in which you parallel your interpretation of a particular artwork or artist with events going on in the world around you.

3. Write an essay in which you parallel your interpretation of a particular artwork or artist with events unfolding in your own life.

4. Think about a film that you love, that you could watch any number of times. Look closely at the conventions and physical experience of film, and question your obsession. In what ways are you comforted by the artifice of film? Where do you suspend your sense of its unreality and where do you take comfort in it? Where did you first see the film, and what has it represented to the larger cul-

ture? If you like, you can substitute something from television, but for this exercise you should go for a quality piece.

5. Think about television commercials that stick with you. How do they define the eras they appear in? How have they shaped you, perhaps in terms of social relationships, signs of status, body image?

6. Write a review of a film or a television show, using specific details that reveal your own voice and vision and that place the show in a larger context.

7. Write an essay that uses popular television or radio shows to establish the time and place of your piece. What were the shows you watched as a child? How did they establish the routine of your day? Why do you think those particular shows hooked you?

8. This prompt expands on uses of music presented in Chapter 1. Identify the piece of music that's been most important to you in your life. First, try to write down why it means so much to you, and when and where you can remember hearing it. If there are lyrics, write down all you can remember, and list adjectives that describe the melody.

   Now try tracing all of the cultural connections of the song, as the authors of *Strange Fruit* did. This may or may not take a little bit of research.

9. Try to imagine your way into the head of a musician you love. Create a speculative narrative that combines fact and fiction to bring that person's music to life on the page.

10. Think about your reading life. What piece of writing has "taken the top of your head off," to use Emily Dickinson's phrase? Write a reading narrative in which you enter into dialogue with this writing—feel free to quote it. How has this reading experience changed you and helped you to redefine your life and your mission as a writer?

11. Write a history of your life through the books you've read. What was your favorite book at age five? Age ten? Age sixteen? Age twenty? Write these out in sections, rendering in specific, sensory detail the memories these books inspire in you.

7

Writing the Larger World

Like Flemish miniaturists who reveal the essence of humankind
within the confines of a tiny frame, McPhee once again demonstrates
that the smallest topic is replete with history, significance, and
consequence.

—FROM A REVIEW OF JOHN
McPHEE'S *ORANGES*

*The first nonfiction book I remember reading and going back to read again
was Lewis Thomas's* The Lives of a Cell. *I read it while sitting in my little rented room in Arcata, California; I was a senior in college, a nascent
Buddhist brimming with questions about the world and my place in it.
Thomas had me thinking about mitochondria—mitochondria!—and the
topic had called into question every perception I thought was sound. No
longer was I a separate organism, contained within my skin, but a mere
continuance of a single cell that erupted eons ago in the primordial soup.*

*What got to me about these "Notes of a Biology Watcher" was not the
information itself (had I read the same information in the encyclopedia I
doubt it would have affected me so), but how that information was presented. Thomas was no mere biologist, but a philosopher and a poet; his sensibility permeated the information and made it real, made it personable.
As I became more and more interested in creative nonfiction, I found this
same kind of voice in many of the writers I loved: E. B. White, John
McPhee, Tom Wolfe, Joan Didion, to name just a few. These authors*

brought their "I" to the world, without becoming self-centered; their focus often remained determinedly outward without sacrificing the voice that made their work unique.

Recently, National Public Radio aired a story about the recent spate in nonfiction books that focus on topics one might not expect to find interesting: orchids, tulips, mosquitoes, clouds, ether, and something as diminutive and common as dust. People are reading these books on the bus, at the beach, in a chair by the window; they're coming to the breakfast table and saying to their loved ones, "Did you know about . . . ?"

—BRENDA

Turning Outward: Finding Your Material Outside the Self

Your own private world—if you inhabit it long enough—will become claustrophobic, not only for yourself but also for your readers. In Chapters 5 and 6, we showed how placing yourself in the contexts of history or art can help diffuse some of the inward-focus of creative nonfiction. In this chapter, we encourage you to direct your gaze outward, not leaving the self behind but perhaps sublimating the self to newly discover the subjects the world has to offer.

Lee Gutkind, founder and editor of the journal *Creative Nonfiction*, believes that one of the genre's essential missions is "to gather and present information, to teach readers about a person, place, idea or situation combining the creativity of the artistic experience with . . . research. . . . Read the books and essays of the most renowned nonfiction writers in this century and you will read about a writer engaged in a quest for information and discovery."

A good creative nonfiction writer will be attuned to the things of the world that beckon for examination. In this chapter, we've broken down the categories into a few that interest us, but as with all the prompts we provide in this book, these are mere gateways for your own creative instincts.

Science

A friend said recently that every time he opens up a newspaper these days he reads something that hits his view of the world with a thunderbolt: Stephen Hawking announces that we must use genetic engineering to evolve faster or computers will make us extinct; there may be infinite parallel universes; a religious group is working to clone human beings.

When you write about science in creative nonfiction, it becomes much more than a recitation or analysis of facts but a means of probing the deepest levels of our common existence. Right now we live steeped in startling scientific and technological advances. These changes signal more than quirky facts to recite; they invade our deepest assumptions about who we are. Here's where literary nonfiction writers become almost essential for our very survival.

We need Lewis Thomas to help us take in the infinite complexities science has found in cell behavior. We need Ursula Goodenough (also a cell biologist), who in her *The Sacred Depths of Nature* creates a sophisticated theology out of an examination of cellular life. We need Oliver Sacks, writing books like *The Man Who Mistook His Wife for a Hat*, to teach us how humans cope and remain whole while a myriad of neurological forces buffet them. Michael Pollan, in *The Botany of Desire*, plants genetically modified potatoes in his garden and maps out the exact nature of genetic modification and its implications for agriculture, as well as how it feels to grow these potatoes, classified by the EPA as "pesticides," not food. (Hint: he doesn't eat them.) Writer-scientists like Stephen Hawking take us by the hand through a changing cosmos that barely makes sense to physicists now.

The Layperson's Approach. Many personal essayists, such as Annie Dillard, draw heavily on scientific knowledge without being classified as science writers, per se. These authors may flesh out a personal experience with facts that enrich the narrative and that may also be alive with metaphoric significance. Dillard's well-known essay "Total Eclipse" begins with the bald declaration, "It had been like dying, that sliding down the mountain pass." She approaches this experience with a voice that is personal and vulnerable. She writes of the experience of a total eclipse as something that continually threatens to overwhelm her and the other onlookers. The intensity of her reactions ("God save our life," "the last sane moment I remember") continues to emphasize that vulnerability. This passion is matched by that of the cosmos she constantly fits herself into, one in which light and darkness exist in a constant dance of existence and extinguishing.

The Ring Nebula, in the constellation Lyra, looks, through binoculars, like a smoke ring. It is a star in the process of exploding. Light from its explo-

sion first reached the earth in 1054; it was a supernova then, and so bright it shone in the daytime. Now it is not so bright, but it is still exploding.

Because Dillard insists on switching back to the world of cosmic activity from the world of human activity, we see her sense of being "obliterated" by the eclipse as a coherent response to a cosmos where darkness can signal an ultimate end. Hers becomes a thinking reaction to the universe we're tied to so intimately.

The Expert's Approach. Richard Selzer's perspective is different. He is an essayist and also a practicing surgeon, and rather than recording his own vulnerability in his essay "The Knife," he records the fearful power his practitioner's skills give him. Selzer implies again and again that perhaps no human is fully equipped to have the life-and-death power of the surgeon: "A stillness settles in my heart and is carried to my hand. It is the quietude of resolve layered over fear." As he operates, he records the following: "Deeper still. The peritoneum, pink and gleaming and membranous, bulges into the wound. It is grasped with forceps, and opened. For the first time we can see into the cavity of the abdomen. Such a primitive place."

Selzer performs a matching "surgery" on his own emotions, delving deeper and deeper into the emotional and philosophical aspects of his role. "Here is man as microcosm, representing in all his parts the earth, perhaps the universe." Or: "And if the surgeon is like a poet, then the scars you have made on countless bodies are like verses."

You don't have to be a veteran of the surgical theater to have a topic you can approach as an informed voice. If you have mastered computer technology, been part of a field camp, dissected something, or learned to fix a car, you have a subject you can write about with both expertise and poetry.

Sports Writing

It is astonishing how much we reveal about ourselves, personally and as a society, through sports. Think of the social implications of being a "tomboy" or a "klutz," then think of the way sports figures embody our cultural idealizations. There's a reason a great basketball player or Olympic gymnast can use his or her image to sell almost any product going. Reflecting about sports has yielded much great writing on the topics of our societal concepts of success and failure, masculinity and femininity, and race, as well as a way of experiencing through words one of life's great visceral excitements.

David Halberstam, one of the editors of *The Best American Sports Writing of the Century*, describes the sports writing he presents as a portrait "of the nation itself during the explosive period" of the twentieth century. His coeditor Glenn Stout calls ours a "golden age" of sports writing. Both editors—seasoned writers themselves—credit the upsurge in this form to authors like Gay Talese and Tom Wolfe, who refused to sacrifice breadth and literary flair in their sports journalism. As Stout puts it, describing the Best American Sports Writing series, "at least once or twice in every edition it was proven, unquestionably, that the best 'sports writing' was . . . just good writing that happened to be about sports." Keep this in mind as you go through the exercises at the end of this chapter. Think about how your own sports obsessions reflect yourself and your culture and what larger questions—of race, violence, and gender—come into play in the sport you choose to write about.

Joyce Carol Oates's book *On Boxing* uses the sport to reflect on larger questions. Sports writing is a field still dominated by men; it's a little surprising to see a woman writing about sports, especially such a traditionally masculine sport as boxing. She begins the essay by complicating this kind of masculinity:

> *No sport is more physical, more direct, than boxing. No sport appears more powerfully homoerotic: the confrontation in the ring—the disrobing—the sweaty heated combat that is part dance, courtship, coupling—the frequent urgent pursuit by one boxer of the other in the fight's natural and violent movement toward the "knockout."*

Oates punctures most readers' basic beliefs about boxing, using specific observations of movements in the ring—movements mirrored by her jumpy, fragmented writing—to do so. She observes the embrace the fighters exchange after the fight and goes on to ask, "Are men privileged to embrace with love only after having fought?" Oates makes the bold statement that this proves man's greatest passion "is for war, not peace." You might disagree with her conclusions, but the essay uses a close observation of a sport Oates loves to ask questions about gender roles, the nature of love and intimacy, and our human instincts.

The Myriad Things Around Us

Can you imagine writing an entire book about a color? The writing of the *Oxford English Dictionary*? The flight path of a single type of butterfly? How about those clingy grains you thoughtlessly shake off your feet at the beach? Lovely, profound, and popular books have been published in the last few years about such seemingly small things.

Poet Theodore Roethke wrote, "All finite things reveal infinitude." William Blake wrote "To see a world in a grain of sand, / and heaven in a wild flower." These thoughts are not just poets' ideas but philosophical truths nonfiction writers have been among the most successful at plumbing. On the one hand, Annie Dillard's *For the Time Being* is a book about everything, and, on the other hand, a book about—sand. At least sand—a solid substance that flows and functions like water—forms a starting point for her long theological look at the flux of the world, Hasidism, and God.

OK, you might say, perhaps sand is interesting, but color? As Simon Garfield, author of *Mauve: How One Man Invented a Color That Changed the World*, discovers, mauve had a lasting impact on the culture of its day (and ours). The color was discovered by an eighteen-year-old chemistry student, who found it in a test tube in the course of trying out something else. The first synthetic color, mauve soon became a status symbol flaunted by royals, including Queen Victoria. (Contemporaries decried the aristocratic passion for mauve by calling streets pocked by wearers as having a case of "mauve measles.") And, naturally, the invention of synthetic color changed the textile industry and the economies of the day.

Hindus speak reverently of "Indra's net"—a web of interconnectedness with a jewel at each intersection that can be used to embody the interconnectedness of the world. Gifted writers like Dillard and Garfield find the "webs" attached to the subjects that draw them—the flowing and flux suggested by sand, the accident of a test-tube residue changing the fashions and industry of a nineteenth-century imperial power.

As a writer, once you begin to look closely at what's around you—recognizing both the closest details and the larger ways each thing fits into the "Indra's net" that holds us all together—nothing will seem less than a fruitful subject for your writing.

The Essay of Ideas

The essay has long been *the* form for exploring the workings of the human intellect. Running the gamut from argument to rumination, authors have always used the essay as a vehicle for both developing and expressing ideas, holding political debates, and delving into personal philosophy. Many of us have bad memories of writing "themes" in high school; the five-paragraph essay that rigidly prescribed the way an intellectual essay could work: thesis, three supporting paragraphs, and a tepid conclusion. Here, in the realm of creative nonfiction, you can redeem the essay of ideas and return it to its rightful place in the literary arts.

As with all good creative nonfiction, it's important to make the essay specific to you and your particular voice. Writing about abstract concepts does not need to be dull or dry; on the contrary, here is an opportunity for you to use the techniques of vivid writing to illuminate difficult and obscure topics. You will seek to uncover the scenes, the details, the images, and the metaphors that make for a memorable essay.

For example, in the essay "The Semiotics of Sex," Jeanette Winterson begins a highly complex discussion of aesthetics, art, and ideology with a scene in a bookstore:

> *I was in a bookshop recently when a young woman approached me.*
> *She told me she was writing an essay on my work and that of Radclyffe Hall. Could I help?*
> *"Yes," I said. "Our work has nothing in common."*
> *"I thought you were a lesbian," she said.*

With this brief scene, Winterson provides a compelling example that wholeheartedly admits the "I" into the intellectual discussion to follow. Rather than dryly elucidate her thesis in the first paragraph, *then* provide a support for that thesis, she does the opposite; she finds a scene that encapsulates her argument and she renders that scene in a way that reveals her personality, her voice, and her concerns.

It is the combination of a personal urgency with intellectual musings that makes the essay of ideas thrive. Remember "Notes of a Native Son" from

Chapter 5? Baldwin focuses on the death of his father, but issues of race and violence pulse through the essay, creating a political argument much more effective than any pundit's analysis.

Paradoxically, when you write about abstract concepts—ideas—it is even more important to pay attention to the concrete details that make such things comprehensible. The good essay of ideas will be a mix of argument and reflection—knowledge and experience—so that in the end the reader has gained some insight into both the ideas and the mind behind them.

TRY IT

1. Scientific facts are often rich in metaphor, as is scientific language. Great science writing draws the material facts of the universe into the process of reflection on the human experience. How would it inform your writing to know that doctors call the two coverings of the brain the "hard mother" (dura mater) and the "tender mother" (pia mater)? How does it change your sense of your own experience to know that physicists believe there may be an infinite number of parallel universes, containing what ours contains, in somewhat different form?

To speed you in the process of exploring the metaphorical value of scientific facts, do a twenty-minute freewrite on any of the following bits of information. Write whatever associations or suggestions come into your head. Which of your own experiences crop up when you think of these facts?

- The human body contains a vestigial tailbone.
- Our galaxy contains a black hole into which our solar system, including earth, will ultimately collapse.
- Stephen Hawking has said that if humans don't begin to use genetic engineering to modify themselves—including incorporating computer technology—computers will evolve past us and possibly cause our extinction.
- Clones are, for little-known reasons, abnormally large.

Before you begin your freewriting session, whether in a class or a writing group or alone, add to this list any facts that have stuck in your mind as suggestive, fascinating, or just bizarre.

After your freewriting session, assuming the material interests you, try expanding it into an essay this way: use a human story (it can be your own or someone else's) to intersperse with the scientific material. At some point in the essay, you must expand on the science, but promise yourself it will not dominate.

2. Identify an area of expertise you have. (We *all* have them!) Detail that work, as Richard Selzer does so carefully in "The Knife." Examine your role and the larger significance of it, as well as the role this specialized activity plays in human culture and your own life. Think of how it makes you feel, what aspect of your humanity it accentuates.

3. Examine a sport in terms of the imagery of its body movements, dress, rituals, and rules. Do any of these seem to defy our stereotypes of this sport? What social significance can you draw from what you see? How do you connect to this sport emotionally?

4. Think of a way in which a sport has had significance in your own life or that of someone close to you. Are there ways in which this personal experience and the sport, or a sports player's career, have run parallel? How? Can you think of a time when a sporting event had an emotional impact on an important event in your own life?

5. Freewrite a list of things you deal with on a daily basis and don't think about very much. Don't be choosy; jot down whatever pops into your head. paper, fluorescent lighting, mosquitoes, slugs, flush toilets. Then select one item from your list.

What are the larger metaphysical (that is, dealing with the properties of the universe at large) connotations of your item? Look at it if you can. Let's say you have chosen a piece of white paper. What does your paper suggest? What are the implications of its smoothness and whiteness? Of writing on pressed trees? Of writing within a square frame? Don't censor yourself but simply go with your impulses. Be weird. Be funny. Find the universe in the particular "grain of sand" in front of you.

Next, uncover a few facts about your item. They may be things you already know, or that classmates or group members can tell you (having a group discussion can really launch a great freewrite here; we trivia buffs are many!) or that you can look up quickly on the Internet. (See Chapter 11, "The Basics of Personal Reportage," if you're stymied.) Then do a second freewrite, focusing on details about your item that feel interesting or suggestive. Again, don't censor yourself. Feel free to be silly, and to be broad.

6. Make a list of the abstract concepts on which you have some opinions: racism, politics, gender wars, and so forth. Now circle one of these, and come up with a list of some specific examples from your own experience that elucidate these abstract concepts in a concrete way. How can you gain *authority* to talk about these issues? How can you demonstrate to the reader that you have firsthand knowledge of these topics?

7. Collect newspaper stories and magazine articles that strike you over the course of a few weeks. Gather these headlines together and begin to explore *why* these particular stories grab your attention. Begin to do a little research on the details of these stories to see if they could lead to a larger essay.

PART 2

THE FORMS OF
CREATIVE NONFICTION

The best work speaks intimately to you even though it has been consciously made to speak intimately to thousands of others. The bad writer believes that sincerity of feeling will be enough, and pins her faith on the power of experience. The true writer knows that feeling must give way to form. It is through the form, not in spite of, or accidental to it, that the most powerful emotions are let loose over the greatest number of people.

—JEANETTE WINTERSON

8

The Particular Challenges
of Creative Nonfiction

Of course a picture can lie, but only if you yourself are not honest or
if you don't have enough control over your subject. Then it is the
camera working, not you.

—ANDRÉ KERTÉSZ,
PHOTOGRAPHER

*I'm writing an essay about my grandmother. I'm not sure why I'm writing
this; there are just certain scenes and images that haunt me and I have to
get them down on paper: my grandmother immobilized in a hospital bed,
the ties of her hospital gown undone around her collarbone; my mother crying quietly in a restaurant as she tells me she can't bring herself to care for
her mother in her home. As I write, I have to make several questionable
choices: do I really remember massaging my grandmother's back that day in
the hospital? Now that I've written it, the scene's taken on the stamp of truth,
seems to have replaced any "real" memories I might have of that day. And
do I relate the scene of my mother's shame; is it really my story to tell? Can
I imagine a scene between my mother and my grandmother, the difficulty
of touch between them?*

*In the end, several months later, I decide to leave in the massage scene—
it has an emotional truth to it, a resonance that indicates to me the memory is valid, not only for the essay but for myself. But I delete the scene with
my mother in the restaurant; though the facts of this moment are more readily verifiable, I've decided that it oversteps some boundary I've set up for*

73

myself. That part is not my story to tell—I don't have the authority or the permission—and it feels too risky. I also, therefore, need to cut the scene where I imagine my mother and grandmother together in our family home. This is a difficult cut—I love the writing in that section—but it needs to go because the scene no longer fits in with the trajectory of the essay.

Yet I know that none of this writing has been wasted. Through writing the scenes I eventually eliminated, I came to understand what was important for this particular essay: to focus my attention on the metaphors of touch, the difficulties of such simple gestures within the family. I also learned how I draw the theoretical lines for myself, how I choose to go about negotiating the ethical land mines of creative nonfiction.

—BRENDA

Find Your Form—Find Your Slant

We began this book with a nod to Emily Dickinson and her mandate to "tell all the truth but tell it slant." Part 1, we hope, has helped you find out just what kinds of "truths" you may have to offer. Now your job is to find a way to "tell it slant," to find the forms that will contain these truths in the most effective and interesting ways. As a writer of creative nonfiction, you must continually make artistic choices that will finesse life's experience into art that will have lasting meaning for others.

Through a careful attention to form, you will be able to create art out of your own experience. Understanding *how* we are structuring our experience forces us to be concrete and vivid. Ironically, the more particular you make your own experience—with sensory details, compelling metaphors, and luscious rhythms—the more fully a reader will feel the personal story along with you. By experiencing it, the reader begins to *care* about it, because your experience has now become his own.

We hope that you will come to find that form is your friend; that by placing your allegiance in artifact over experience, the material becomes just that: raw material that you will use to fashion art, rather than the intractable stuff of memory and experience. To come back to our friend Emily Dickinson, in a letter to Thomas Higginson, she said, rather cryptically, "My business is circumference." By this she means perhaps that she circled her life, encompassing every hummingbird, every fly, every bit of bread into her art. All creative nonfiction writers should take heed. Observe your life from every angle—

cocking your head, squinting your eyes—then fashion what you see through a voice that is yours and yours alone. Tell us the truth, but shape it in a way that wakes us from our doldrums and startles us into a new grasp of our strange and remarkable lives.

A Few Caveats About Writing from Life

Creative nonfiction is a tricky business. On the one hand, you have the challenge—and the thrill—of turning real life into art. But on the other hand, you have to deal with all the issues that come attached with that "real life." When a fiction writer wants her character to remember the first time she ate ice cream, she can enter the problem imaginatively: place the character at Coney Island with a melting chocolate cone or at a birthday party with a neat scoop on a slice of cake. Can you do the same thing when you're writing from your own memory, even when you don't exactly remember the scene? A fiction writer is able to create the set amount of characters necessary for the story's action; can you do the same thing with the characters you encounter in your own life and research? When a fiction writer needs dialogue, she writes dialogue. As a nonfiction writer, can you make up dialogue you don't remember verbatim? When you're writing essays based on research, how much of your imagination can you use? Does "nonfiction" mean "no fiction"?

The self inhabits the prose of creative nonfiction, whether or not you write directly about your own experiences. It is this "I" that picks and chooses among the facts. This "I" re-creates those essential scenes and makes crucial decisions about what to include and what to exclude. The "I" decides on the opening line that will set up the voice of the piece, the essential themes and metaphors. The "I" gives the essay its *personality*, both literally and figuratively. The essential question, then, is how do you create a piece inhabited by the self without becoming self-centered? And how do you negotiate all the ethical and technical obstacles that come with writing from real life?

The "I" and the Eye: Framing Experience

A useful way of looking at how creative nonfiction employs the "I" is to align the genre with photography. Both photography and creative nonfiction operate under the "sign of the real" (a phrase coined by literary theorist Hayden White); both operate *as though* the medium itself were transparent. In other words, when you look at a photograph, you are lulled into the illusion that you see the world as it is—looking through a window, as it were—but in reality you are being shown a highly manipulated version of that world. The same is true with creative nonfiction. Because it operates under the sign of the real, it can be easy to mistake the essay as presenting life itself, without adulteration.

But both photography and creative nonfiction actually function just as subjectively as fiction and painting, because the personal "eye" is the mechanism for observation, and the inner "I" is the medium through which these observations are filtered. As Joan Didion puts it, "No matter how dutifully we record what we see around us, the common denominator of all we see is always, transparently, shamelessly, the implacable 'I.'" The minute you begin to impose form on experience—no matter how dutifully you try to remain faithful to history or the world—you're immediately faced with a technical dilemma: how do you effectively frame this experience? What gets left outside the confines of this frame? Are some frames more "truthful" than others? And the way you decide to frame the world directly reflects the "I" and the "eye" that perform this act of construction.

Wallace Stegner, in his book *Where the Bluebird Sings to the Lemonade Springs*, posits that our task as writers is "to write a story, though ignorant or baffled. You take something that is important to you, something you have brooded about. You try to see it as clearly as you can, and to fix it in a transferable equivalent. All you want in the finished print is the clean statement of the lens, *which is yourself*, [emphasis ours] on the subject that has been absorbing your attention." A good photograph will mirror the inner vision of the photographer, just as a good essay will reflect the unique sensibility of the writer, whether or not that writer focuses on material interior to the self.

The Persona of the First-Person Narrator

Just as the details of the world and experience may be framed or constructed by a mediating "I," so too is that "I" a fabrication for the purposes of the essay. We are not the same on the page as we are in real life, and we must be aware that the "I" is just as much a tool—or a point of view or a character—that we manipulate for particular effects. The "I" on the page is really a fictional construction, reflecting certain parts of us, leaving others out, or exaggerating certain aspects for the purposes of the essay at hand.

For instance, Bernard Cooper is not *always* obsessed with the sound of sighs, as he is in his essay "The Fine Art of Sighing," just as David James Duncan often has other things on his mind besides the baseball sent to his brother the day after the brother died, which he describes in his essay "The Mickey Mantle Koan." But, for the time span of the essay, they create themselves as characters with these obsessions that focus the piece and create its reason for existing at all.

In *The Situation and the Story*, memoirist Vivian Gornick writes about finding her voice in creative nonfiction. "I began to read the greats in essay writing—and it wasn't their confessing voices I was responding to, it was their truth-speaking personae," she writes. "I have created a persona who can find the story riding the tide that I, in my unmediated state, am otherwise going to drown in." The narrating "I," the persona you create, is the one who has the wherewithal to rescue experience from chaos and turn it into art.

The Pact with the Reader

As you create this persona, you also establish a relationship between yourself and the reader. In creative nonfiction—more so, perhaps, than in any other genre—readers assume a real person behind the artifice, an author who *speaks* directly to the reader. Just as in spoken conversations, it's a symbiotic relationship. The reader completes this act of communication through his attention to the author's story, and the author must establish right away a reason for the reader to be attentive at all. For this relationship to work, however, the author must establish a certain level of trust.

Simply presenting your work as an "essay" rather than a piece of fiction sets up certain assumptions. The reader will be engaged in a "true story," one rooted in the world as we know it. Because of this assumption, the reader needs to know he is in good hands, in the presence of, in Vivian Gornick's words, a "truth-speaking" guide who will lead him somewhere worthwhile. The reader needs to know he won't be deceived along the way, led to believe something that turns out to be patently untrue. Philippe Lejeune, in his sem-

inal work *On Autobiography*, calls this the "pact with the reader." The essayist pledges, in some way, both to be as honest as possible with the reader *and*
to make this conversation worthwhile. Without this pact, true communication becomes impossible.

As essayist Patricia Hampl puts it, "You tell me your story, I'll tell you
mine." Without this understanding, we become more like the people you
occasionally see in the park: men and women talking to themselves, rehash-
ing past wrongs, their arms gesticulating wildly in the air. We don't really *listen* to such a narrator; in fact our impulse is to turn and walk in the opposite
direction.

So, *how* does a writer establish this kind of pact with the reader? In the
introduction to *The Art of the Personal Essay*, essayist Phillip Lopate writes
that "part of our trust in good personal essayists issues, paradoxically, from
their exposure of their own betrayals, uncertainties, and self-mistrust." When
we reveal our own foibles, readers can relax and know they engage in conversation with someone as human as they are.

Good writers can also establish this pact through their skillful manipula-
tion of the techniques that make for vivid writing (see Chapter 12). If we know
we are in the hands of a literary artist—one who won't let us down with
clichés or a weak infrastructure—then we're usually willing to go wherever
he or she leads. We assume that the writer has shaped the material for its best
literary effect, while at the same time remaining as true as possible to the
"facts" of the world and history. Let's take a look at some famous essayists and
see how they establish a pact with the reader early on in their work, combining craft with content:

> **Joan Didion ("Goodbye to All That"):** "That first night I opened
> my window on the bus into town and watched for the skyline, but all
> I could see were the wastes of Queens and the big signs that said
> MIDTOWN TUNNEL THIS LANE and then a flood of summer
> rain (even that seemed remarkable and exotic, for I had come out of
> the West where there was no summer rain), and for the next three
> days I sat wrapped in blankets in a hotel room air-conditioned to 35°
> and tried to get over a bad cold and a high fever. It did not occur to
> me to call a doctor, because I knew none, and although it did occur
> to me to call the desk and ask that the air conditioner be turned off, I

never called, because I did not know how much to tip whoever might come—was anyone ever so young? I am here to tell you that someone was."

E. B. White ("Afternoon of an American Boy"): "Seeing him, I would call 'Hello, Parnell!' and he would smile and say 'Hello, Elwyn!' and walk on. Once I remember dashing out of our yard on roller skates and executing a rink turn in front of Parnell, to show off, and he said, 'Well, quite an artist, aren't you?' I remember the words. I was delighted at praise from an older man and sped away along the flagstone sidewalk, dodging the cracks I knew so well."

Margaret Atwood ("Nine Beginnings"): "1. *Why do you write?* I've begun this piece nine times. I've junked every beginning. I hate writing about my writing. I almost never do it. Why am I doing it now? Because I said I would. I got a letter. I wrote back *no*. Then I was at a party and the same person was there. It's harder to refuse in person. Saying yes had something to do with being nice, as women are taught to be, and something to do with being helpful, which we are also taught."

Bernard Cooper ("The Fine Art of Sighing"): "You feel a gradual welling up of pleasure, or boredom, or melancholy. Whatever the emotion, it's more abundant than you ever dreamed. You can no more contain it than your hands can cup a lake. And so you surrender and suck the air. Your esophagus opens, diaphragm expands. Poised at the crest of an exhalation, your body is about to be unburdened, second by second, cell by cell. A kettle hisses. A balloon deflates. Your shoulders fall like two ripe pears, muscles slack at last."

What do you find in common with these four very different essayists? Though they write about quite divergent subjects, and from widely varying points of view, they've all constructed an "I" voice that speaks directly to the reader, and they all give the reader some evidence that it will be worthwhile to remain in this conversation. In her long, breathless sentences, Joan Didion reveals her embarrassment and timidity at being in a city where she knows no one and is unsure of the social conventions. Not only does she reel us in because of the details (we get to be on that bus with her), but she also laughs at herself and invites the reader to laugh with her. "Was anyone ever so young? I am here to tell you someone was." These two sentences establish that Didion has perspective on her experience. She has garnered some wisdom in the time between then and now, and so we won't be subjected to a rendition of raw emotion; rather the material will be shaped and presented by someone who is able to distance herself from the "I" who is a character in her story, and the "I" who narrates that story many years later.

E. B. White gains our trust because he is able to vividly describe a scene of childish delight and in such a way that we experience it along with him. Though we may never have had White's exact experience, he keys us into an experience that might be termed universal. Surely we've all experienced some moment of joy such as his, some moment when we were recognized by someone we admired. And if we haven't, White makes us wish we had, with his strong verbs ("dashing," "executing," "dodging"), and his powerful sentence structure that leaps and dodges and ends in a sigh of nostalgic satisfaction. White, like Didion, also shows us that he understands the difference between creating an "I" character in the story and a narrating "I" with the skills to render this story effectively. The line "I remember the words," while deceptively simple and commonplace, alerts the reader to the older writer's presence in the scene, looking on and rediscovering it along with the reader.

Margaret Atwood uses the form itself to establish that we're in good hands. She uses the interview question as a reason for writing in the first place, and then confesses that she'd rather do anything but write the essay we have in our hands. The tension between the question (which recurs nine times throughout the essay, an insistent voice that spurs the writer and reader on) and her tentative answers to that question, provide dramatic suspense for an essay that could easily, in other hands, become clichéd or predictable. Also, by confessing her difficulty with writing, she allows us to relate to her experience. It's as though she's giving voice to the doubts we all carry in our heads, a daring move that we silently applaud. She creates a persona, forthright and strong, who is able to say the things we ourselves might find difficult.

Bernard Cooper reaches out a hand and tugs us into his essay by starting off with the second-person point of view. "You feel a gradual welling up of pleasure." He makes us a participant in his essay by re-creating a sigh on the page. Read the passage aloud and see if you can keep from letting out a long, hearty sigh. And the "you" makes an assertion that's difficult to deny. The experience he creates on the page does indeed become a universal sigh, exhaled in common with thousands of others.

All these writers, along with the multitude of creative nonfiction writers we admire, must immediately make a case for taking up a reader's time and attention. In doing so, they also take care of the "so what?" question that plagues writers of creative nonfiction and of memoir in particular. Why should anyone care about your personal story or your perspective on the world? What use will the essay have for anyone outside of yourself? By engaging you in their essays through vivid details and an authentic voice, through imaginative uses of form and structure, these essayists show that the personal can indeed become universal. We care about their stories because they have become *our* stories. They have verbalized for us what has previously remained silent or have at least rephrased these issues for us in such a way as to make them new. That's what we're after as readers of literature: a fresh articulation of the world so that we might understand it more thoroughly. These essayists do so through both personal revelation and careful crafting of their prose.

The Permutations of "Truth": Fact Versus Fiction

If you set out to establish a pact with the reader—to gain his or her trust—then you must make some critical decisions about how—or whether—you will employ fictional elements in your nonfiction writing. As we've noted earlier, the simple act of writing and the construction of the narrative voice are essentially creative acts that impose a form where none before existed. Beyond that, what kinds of fictions are allowable and what are not in creative nonfiction? Just how much emphasis do we put on "creative" and how much on "nonfiction"?

Some writers believe that nothing at all should ever be knowingly made up in creative nonfiction. If you can't remember what color dress you wore at your sixth-grade graduation, then you better leave that detail out or do some studied research to find the answer. If you had five best friends in high school who helped you through a jam, then you better not compress those five into one or two composite characters for the sake of efficient narrative. On the other hand, some writers believe that small details can be fabricated to create the scenes of memory, and they knowingly create composite characters because the narrative structures demand it. Some writers willingly admit imagination into factual narratives; others abhor it and see it as a trespass into fiction.

It's interesting to note that when a writer publishes a piece of fiction that contains highly autobiographical elements, no one flinches; in fact, such blurring of the boundaries is often presumed. But to admit fictional techniques into autobiographical work creates controversy and furious discussion. The nature of that essential pact with the reader—that sense of trust—demands this kind of scrutiny into the choices we make as nonfiction writers.

We believe that every writer must negotiate the boundary between fact and fiction for him- or herself. What constitutes fabrication for one writer will seem like natural technique to another. But what we can do here is show how some writers employ fictional techniques and the effects these choices have on your credibility as an essayist.

Memory and Imagination

If your work is rooted in memory, you will find yourself immediately confronted with the imagination. Memory, in a sense, *is* imagination: an "imaging" of the past, re-creating the sights, sounds, smells, tastes, and touches (see Chapter 1). In her essay "Memory and Imagination," Patricia Hampl writes, "I am forced to admit that memoir is not a matter of transcription, that memory itself is not a warehouse of finished stories, not a static gallery of framed pictures. I must admit that I invented. But why?"

We invent because our lives and the world contain more than simple facts; imagination and the way we imagine are as much a part of ourselves as any factual résumé. In creative nonfiction, the creative aspect involves not only writing techniques, but also a creative interpretation of the facts of our lives, plumping the skeletal facts with the flesh of imagination. Personal history sometimes demands this kind of elaboration for its full significance to emerge on the page. Hampl continues, "We find, in our details and broken and obscured images, the language of symbol. Here memory impulsively reaches out its arms and embraces imagination. That is the resort to invention. It isn't a lie, but an act of necessity, as the innate urge to locate personal truth always is."

Look back to the tonsil story that precedes Chapter 1. There's no real way to verify either the fact or fiction of the tonsils floating in a jar on the bed-side table. What I, Brenda, can do with this image is admit the bizarre and unlikely nature of this mental picture that imagination has called forth in con-junction with memory. I can say "Why do I remember this jar of tonsils at my hospital bedside?" In so doing, I readily admit the imagination into mem-ory and can then proceed to construct an essay that both interprets the image for metaphorical significance and allows it to become a jumping-off point for a longer meditation on the topics this metaphor suggest. I do not discount or omit this image because its factual veracity is in question; rather I relish the opportunity to explore that rich boundary zone between memory and imag-ination. And I do so in full view of my audience, disclosing my intent, and so maintaining my pact with the reader.

Emotional Truth Versus Factual Truth

Mimi Schwartz in "Memoir? Fiction? Where's the Line?" writes, "Go for the emotional truth, that's what matters. Yes, gather the facts by all means. Look at old photos, return to old places, ask family members what they remember, look up time-line books for the correct songs and fashion styles, read old newspapers, encyclopedias, whatever—and then use the imagination to fill in the remembered experience." If we allow imagination into memory, then we are naturally aligning ourselves with a stance toward an emotional or literary truth; this doesn't mean that we discount factual truth altogether, but that it may be important, for *literary* purposes, to fill in what you can of the facts to get at a truth that resonates with a different kind of veracity on the page. Facts only take us so far.

Schwartz continues, "It may be 'murky terrain,' you may cross the line into fiction and have to step back reluctantly into what really happened—the struggle creates the tensions that makes memoir either powerfully true or hopelessly phony. The challenge of this genre is that it hands you characters, plot and setting, and says, 'Go figure them out!'—using fact, memory, and imagination to re-create the complexity of real moments, big and small, with no invented rapes or houses burning down." Here, Schwartz herself draws the line. We may reconstruct certain details, imagine ourselves into the stories *behind* the facts, but certain facts, such as a rape or a house burning down, cannot be invented. Or as novelist and memoirist Bret Lott puts it in his essay "Against Technique," "In fiction you get to make up what happens; in creative nonfiction you don't get to mess with what happen*ed*."

Take a look at the case of a highly publicized memoir, *Fragments: Memories of a Wartime Childhood*. In this lyrical narrative told from a child's point of view, Binjamin Wilkomirski re-creates scenes from his experience as a child survivor of the Holocaust. He recounts his father's execution in graphic detail, scenes of rats scurrying over piles of corpses. The prose is beautifully rendered, and some scenes move the reader to tears. But shortly after publication of this memoir, critics began to question Wilkomirski's veracity. One journalist did some investigation and found evidence that showed the writer had never been in a concentration camp at all. Birth certificates and adoption records showed him born in Switzerland in 1941 and adopted into a family shortly thereafter. However, Wilkomirski stood by his memories which were recovered, he said, in therapy. To him, these memories were as real—they carried just as much emotional truth—as the factual history.

Few people would argue that Wilkomirski hadn't crossed that ethical line for creative nonfiction. Though we've presented arguments that claim emotional truths can be just as veracious as facts, it is not acceptable to appropriate or wholly invent a history that has little or no relation to your own. You still need to use your own history as a scaffolding for the emotional truths you will uncover. While *Fragments* exemplifies this dictum in fairly obvious terms (to appropriate something as horrific and emotionally charged as the Holocaust leaves little room for debate), you need to see how it might operate in smaller ways within your own nonfiction writing. There are facts and then there are *facts*. Which ones are hard and fast?

For example, Annie Dillard has been brought to task simply for claiming to own a cat she never had. Her book *Pilgrim at Tinker Creek* begins with the line "I used to have a cat, an old fighting tom, who would jump through the open window by my bed in the middle of the night and land on my chest." Later in the paragraph she writes, "And some mornings I'd wake in daylight to find my body covered with paw prints in blood; I looked as though I'd been painted with roses." This image becomes important to her spiritual explorations throughout the book, and nowhere does she really acknowledge that the cat is a literary device or a fiction constructed for this purpose. For many readers, this constitutes a breach of contract; though Dillard uses the fictional cat to good effect, the fact that she has deceived the audience in some way undermines her credibility for the rest of the book. "How can we be sure of anything she says from here on out?" these readers would cry. Other readers are willing to exonerate Dillard for this fiction, claiming that it is not an important detail, and the cat is meant as a metaphorical device. After all, the book's subtitle is *A Mystical Excursion into the Natural World.* In the realm of mysticism, even nonexistent fighting toms might materialize to be our spirit guides.

What do you think? Where do you draw the line for your own work? Does Dillard undermine her pact with the reader? Would you be comfortable inserting such fictions in your own nonfiction writing?

"The Whole Truth?"

Sometimes you'll be troubled not by "facts" that are made up, but by those that are omitted. In essay writing, it's nearly impossible to tell the "whole" truth. Of necessity, you'll find yourself needing to pare away certain details, events, and characters to create an essay that makes narrative sense. For example, if you're writing about something that happened in school when you were ten years old, you'll have to decide just how many members of your fifth grade class will make it onto the stage. Who is important and who is not, for this particular essay?

This is an easy one: you'll naturally choose to flesh out the one or two characters closest to you at the time. More difficult will be knowing when and how to omit the characters that felt important in real life but just get in the way once you land them on the page. For example, Bernard Cooper included his brothers in his early book *Maps to Anywhere*, but when he wrote the essays collected in *Truth Serum*, he made a conscious decision to leave his brothers out. This left him open to criticism from reviewers who said he deceived his audience by implying he was an only child. Here is his reply to them, from his essay "Marketing Memory":

*I had three brothers, all of whom died of various ailments, a sibling his-
tory that strains even my credulity. . . . Very early in the writing of* Truth
Serum *I knew that a book concerned with homosexual awakening would
sooner or later deal with AIDS and the population of friends I've lost to the
disease. . . . To be blunt, I decided to limit the body count in this book in
order to prevent it from collapsing under the threat of death. . . . There is
only so much loss I can stand to place at the center of the daily rumination
that writing requires. . . . Only when the infinite has edges am I capable of
making art.*

"Only when the infinite has edges am I capable of making art." Perhaps
that should be a credo we creative nonfiction writers etch on the walls above
our desks. For that is what we're up to all the time: creating those edges, constructing artful containers that will hold some facts and not others.

These "edges" might also be formed by choosing to create "composite characters," or to compress events in time. A composite character is a fictional construction; the author blends the traits of several characters into one or two,
thereby streamlining both the cast of characters and the narratives needed to
take care of them. Compression of time means that you might conflate anecdotes from several trips home into one composite visit. As a writer and a member of a writing community, you'll want to think about these devices—and
talk about them—to see how they conform to your own writing ethics.

Cueing the Reader

As you continue to develop your own guidelines for the permutations of truth
in creative nonfiction, you'll find that you'll create your own tools for negotiating some of these tricky areas. Some simple ones to keep in mind, however, are *taglines* that let the reader in on what exactly you're up to. Phrases
such as "I imagine," "I would like to believe," "I don't remember exactly, but,"
"I would like to remember," or even a simple "Perhaps," alert the reader to
your artistic agenda. Once you set the terms of the discussion—once you situate the reader in that boundary zone between fact and fiction—then you
most likely will be free to go wherever you wish.

For example, what would have happened if Annie Dillard said "I never owned a fighting tom, but I would like to imagine. . . ." Or she might have disclosed where she received the image: "I once had a friend whose fighting tomcat left paw prints of blood on her chest. I wish I had such a creature. . . ." For Dillard, this kind of tagline may have lessened the literary effect of the passage. But it would certainly diffuse any accusations against her credibility as well.

Cueing the reader can be accomplished even more subtly. If you have trouble writing a scene for a family event because it happened ten years ago, try beginning it with a line like, "This is how my father sounded," or, "This is what Sundays were like at my house." Then watch the pieces fall into place. These statements are unobtrusive, but they make it clear that you're not claiming to provide a verbatim transcript of an event.

Writers can also directly tell the reader what they're up to. Full disclosure lets readers know what we're in for. In a daring move, Lauren Slater titles a book *Lying: A Metaphorical Memoir*. Though this book is full of details that prove to be untrue, notably her descriptions of having epileptic seizures, Slater stands by her work with an obvious defense. The title tells us, quite bluntly, that she's fabricating metaphorical experiences. Though you may or may not buy this as a reader, you can't claim that she didn't warn you.

Pitfalls to Avoid: Revenge Prose and the Therapist's Couch

Ironically, while creative nonfiction can be a tool of self-discovery, you must also have some distance from the self to write effectively. You must know when you are ready to write about certain subjects and when you are not. If you are crying while crafting a piece of nonfiction, the tears will smudge the ink, ultimately making your work unreadable. If your hand shakes with anger while writing, the words will veer wildly across the page with no sense of control or design.

This is not to say that creative nonfiction is devoid of emotion; on the contrary, the most powerful nonfiction is propelled by a sense of urgency, the need to speak about events that touch us deeply, both in our personal history and those that occur in the world around us. The key to successfully writing about these events is *perspective*. Earlier in the chapter, we aligned creative nonfiction with photography. Perspective is the way a photographer chooses to frame and compose her photograph, and it is just as vital when you approach the tough subjects for personal essays. Perspective defines the difference between a journal entry meant only for private venting and the essay designed for public consumption.

As readers, we rarely want to read an essay that smacks either of the therapist's couch or revenge prose. In both cases, the writer has not yet gained enough perspective for wisdom or literature to emerge from experience. In therapist's couch prose, the writer is still weighed down by confusing emotions, or feelings of self-pity, and wants only to share those emotions with the reader. The depth of these emotions does not allow for a literary design to emerge. In revenge prose, the writer's intent seems to be to get back at someone else who has wronged him. The offender does not emerge as a fully developed character but only as a flat, one-dimensional incarnation of his awful deeds. In both cases, it is the writer who comes out looking bad, because he has not stepped back enough from the person or events to gain perspective.

As a writer, it is important for you to start recognizing when you can write about certain material and when you cannot. Perhaps it will take another twenty years before you are fully ready to deal with traumatic events in your childhood. It might take years before you're really able to deal with the breakup of your marriage. Or perhaps you will be able to write about a *small* aspect of the experience, focusing your attention on a particular detail that leads to a larger metaphorical significance outside of the event itself. For instance, remember David James Duncan and his koan of the signed baseball? He deals with the death of his brother years after the fact by focusing his attention on that signed baseball sent to his brother by Mickey Mantle. This baseball leads him to a philosophical rumination on the nature of life itself. This *peripheral vision*—this ability to sidle up to the big issues by way of a side route—is the mark of an accomplished writer, one who has gained enough perspective to use personal experience in the service of a larger literary purpose.

The best writers also show a marked generosity toward the characters in their nonfiction, even those who appear unsympathetic or unredeemable. For example, Terry Tempest Williams, in "The Clan of One-Breasted Women," writes an essay that is clearly fueled by anger, but it does not come across as personally vengeful or mean-spirited. Most of the women in her family died of cancer, an illness that could have been caused by the government's testing of nuclear weapons in her home state. By channeling her energy into research, she shows herself as someone with important information to impart, aside from her own personal history. She creates a metaphor—the clan of one-breasted women—that elevates her own story into a tribal one. By directing her attention to the literary design of her material, she is able to transcend the emotional minefield of that material. "Anger," she has said, "must be channeled so that it becomes nourishing rather than toxic." Her work is passionate, yes, but not shrill in a way that might lose her readers.

The Warning Signs

In your own work, always be on the lookout for sections that seem too weighed down by the emotions from which they spring. Here are some warning signs. Read the piece aloud and see if the prose has momentum. Where does it lag and become plodding? Those are the sections that probably haven't been refined enough to avoid melodrama. And seek out any sections that too directly explore your feelings about an event rather than the event itself. Where do you say words such as "I hated," "I felt so depressed," "I couldn't stand"? The "I" here will become intrusive, repeating itself into infinity: a monologue of old grievances.

If you find yourself telling the reader how to feel—and in a tone that's more like aggrieved chatter at a bar than convincing narrative—then you're probably headed right into revenge prose. You don't want to end up sounding like this, "And then you know what else that no-good jerk did? You won't believe this, even after *I* was the one to put him through medical school, and *I* was the one to bear his children, he says *he* needs some space, can you believe that? Space? What the hell does he need *space* for?" Channel your creative energy, instead, into constructing the scenes, images, and metaphors that will allow the reader to have her own reactions, *apart from the ones you had at the time*. On the page, your life is not just your life anymore; you must put your allegiance now into creating an artifact that will have meaning outside the self.

TRY IT

1. Have an individual or group session in which you plumb your own sense of nonfiction ethics. What would you do and what wouldn't you do? Would you re-create a scene or invent dialogue for someone without a clear cue to the reader? Would you invent a fact? It's useful to proceed in your writing with a defined sense of your own boundaries.

2. Practice writing cueing lines. This can be fun to do in a group, while passing one another's essays around or just writing inventive cueing lines to pass ("If I dreamed this scene, this is how I would dream it.") Sharing ideas will get you in the habit of using cueing lines creatively.

3. Try writing out a memory in scene from the perspective of at least two people who were present (members of your family, perhaps). Get their memory down as accurately as you can by questioning them, and write it as carefully and lovingly as you write your own. Think of this as an exercise in the quirks of individual perspective. If you like the results of this exercise, try juxtaposing pieces of each narrative, alternating the voices, to create a braided essay.

4. Try compressing time by creating one scene out of several similar events. For instance, take moments from several Christmas dinners and create one specific scene that encapsulates all of them. What do you gain and/or lose by doing this to your material?

9

The Personal Essay

After a time, some of us learn (and some more slowly than others)
that life comes down to some simple things. How we love, how alert
we are, how curious we are. Love, attention, curiosity. . . . One way
we learn this lesson is by listening to others tell us true stories of their
own struggles to come to a way of understanding. It is sometimes
comforting to know that others seem to fail as often and as oddly as
we do. . . . And it is even more comforting to have such stories told
to us with *style*, the way a writer has found to an individual
expression of a personal truth.

—Scott Walker, editor, *Essays,*
Memoirs & Reflections

*I am a young woman in college, beginning to write. One day I pick up
Annie Dillard's book* Pilgrim at Tinker Creek. *A book-length, meditative
personal essay,* Pilgrim *documents the speaker's observations of the natural
world around her home in Virginia. It is at once deeply individual, as she
looks at the "rosy, complex" light that fills her kitchen in June, and deeply
philosophical, as she draws everything into relationship with the galaxy that
is "careening" around her. It is a bold book, drawing on the seemingly small
in order to embrace the entire world. More important to me at the time,
the speaker is a young woman in her twenties, the author herself. She's not
speaking with the authoritative male voice I have come to associate with the
essay. She speaks as Annie Dillard, with only the authority of our shared
human experience.*

I was fascinated to learn later that Annie Dillard originally began Pilgrim at Tinker Creek *in the voice of a middle-aged male academic, a metaphysician. She didn't trust her own young woman's voice to engage and convince her audience. Other writers persuaded her to trust her voice and abandon the constructed one, and the book won the Pulitzer Prize, proving that the personal essay form is a broad one. It only requires that you be alert, perceptive and human.*

—SUZANNE

The Personal Essay Tradition

The personal essay is "the way a writer has found to an individual expression of a personal truth." When Scott Walker wrote those words in 1986, the personal essay was making a comeback. The reading public seemed hungry for a form that engages us the way fiction does but that also teaches us something about the way real life works. While the phrase "creative nonfiction" had not yet come into popular use, "personal essay" seemed adequate to convey that sense of combining a personal voice with a factual story.

In the West, scholars often date the essay tradition back to the sixteenth-century French writer Michel de Montaigne. *Essays*, composed in Montaigne's retirement, lay much of the groundwork for what we now think of as the essay style: informal, frank (often bawdy), and associative. His book moves easily from a consideration of the classical author Virgil to pieces like "Of Thumbs." His title *Essays*, playing on the French verb meaning "to try," gives us the term we now use routinely in nonfiction writing. The essay writer "tries out" various approaches to the subject, offering tentative forays into an arena where "truth" can be open for debate.

Phillip Lopate, editor of the historically astute anthology *The Art of the Personal Essay*, puts it this way: "The essayist attempts to surround a something—a subject, a mood, a problematic irritation—by coming at it from all angles, wheeling and diving like a hawk, each seemingly digressive spiral actually taking us closer to the heart of the matter."

Prior to Montaigne, as Lopate's anthology illustrates, plenty of writers worked in what we would now consider a personal essay mode. Just a few examples include Sei Shonagon, a tenth-century Japanese courtesan who created elaborately detailed lists that revealed much about herself and her

place in the Japanese court; the Japanese monk Kenko's meditative ruminations translated as *Essays in Idleness*; or Roman emperor Marcus Aurelius,
whose book *Meditations* embodies an aphoristic essay style, creating pithy
"slogans" as advice to those who will succeed him. The Stoic philosopher
Seneca the Younger and the Greek biographer Plutarch both wrote "essays
in disguise" in the form of letters that ruminated on a range of subjects,
from noise in the marketplace to the proper comportment to maintain in
the face of grief.

After Montaigne, British essayists such as Charles Lamb and William
Hazlitt made the essay form their own. According to Lopate, "it was the
English, rather than Montaigne's own countrymen, who took up his challenge
and extended, refined, and cultivated the essay." Lamb wrote about intensely
personal material. (His sister killed their mother and wounded their father;
Lamb, himself, suffered a nervous breakdown.) But, he used a fictional persona that gave him some distance from his subject. Hazlitt wrote more in the
style of Montaigne, creating essays with titles such as "On Going a Journey"
and "On the Pleasure of Hating." At the same time in America, Thoreau was
writing his journals and *Walden*, works that would form the foundation of
American nature writing taken up by writers such as Edward Abbey and
Annie Dillard.

As an essayist, you should take it upon yourself to study the tradition, not
only for general knowledge but to situate yourself within that literary lineup.
How does your own writing work with or against the stylistic tendencies of
a Joan Didion, say, who in turn has a voice that emerges in direct dialogue
with the voice of essayists such as George Orwell? Lopate's *The Art of the Personal Essay* is a good place to start, but also look at works of your contemporaries to see how the essay is evolving in your own generation. The literary
magazine *Fourth Genre: Explorations in Nonfiction* publishes some of the best
contemporary writers in the form, as do the journals *Creative Nonfiction* and
River Teeth: A Journal of Nonfiction Narrative. You should also avail yourself
of the Best American Essays series. The editor, Robert Atwan, culls a selec-
tion of the strongest essays published by American magazines in each year,
and a guest editor pares those down further to a select few. While we will all
have our own definitions of *best*, it is useful to read these anthologies to see
what your contemporaries are up to. By reading widely, you will learn not
only what is possible, but what has still to be discovered.

You may find, as Lopate has, that "at the core of the essay is the supposition that there is a certain unity to human experience." The personal essay carries the implication that the personal, properly rendered, is universally significant or should be. Montaigne echoes this. "Every man has within himself the entire human condition." At the same time, Lopate writes that "the hallmark of the personal essay is its intimacy. The writer seems to be speaking directly into your ear, confiding everything from gossip to wisdom." These two poles—intimacy of voice and universality of significance—go to the heart of the personal essay tradition. The essay speaks confidingly, as a whispering friend, and these whispers must be made meaningful in a larger context—capturing a piece of larger human experience within the amber of your own.

The Way Essays Work

What makes an essay an essay? How can you recognize one when you see it? When we study fiction writing or poetry, certain elements of form are easy enough to identify, such as plot or character development in short stories or lineation and rhythm in poems. Essays can be analyzed the same way, but the task is complicated by the wide variety of styles and forms encompassed by the term "personal essay." Many of these forms overlap with content, and perhaps you've already experienced several of them in the first section of this book. You've already been writing memoir, for example, when you focus on selected memories for a particular metaphorical or narrative effect. You've already started a nature essay when you described some aspect of the environment around you. Perhaps you've already tried the travel piece or a biographical sketch of someone close to you. Perhaps you've sidled up to the spiritual autobiography or the essay of ideas. All of these are forms, defined more by content than craft.

When we turn our attention to craft, we can begin to see some stylistic qualities that help to define the essay form. In his essay "A Boundary Zone," Douglas Hesse describes the difference between essays and short stories in terms of movement. In any narrative prose piece, some sense of forward movement emerges. Visualized as a horizontal line, this line keeps the story moving forward. Some essays read almost like short stories. In the well-known essay "The Fourth State of Matter" by Jo Ann Beard, the horizontal line is a shooting at the author's workplace at the University of Iowa. She begins the piece before the shooting and continues through the event and its emotional aftermath. Three other strands also propel the essay forward: a dying collie, a divorce, and squirrels inhabiting her attic. All these form miniplots, very much like a short story. She uses dialogue freely and re-creates scene with vivid, specific details. And the essay itself reads like a short story because of the present-tense voice (a narrator), and the sense of horizontal story lines unfolding and intersecting at the same time.

In contrast, a more essaylike narrative might have a stronger vertical line to it, the reflective voice that comments upon the scenes it re-creates. David James Duncan works in this mode. In "The Mickey Mantle Koan," the forward, horizontal line of the narrative—the brother's death—is interrupted, or balanced, by his ruminations on the koan of a signed baseball arriving after his brother's death. This reflective voice runs underneath the horizontal line, creating a sense of movement that delves below the surface of narrative.

Once you begin seeing essays in terms of their movement, you can decide how your own work might fit or work against the categories of personal essay. At one extreme, we have the short-story style that engages us with plot, subplots, and scenes. At the other extreme is the analytic meditation that engages us through the power of the writer's interior voice. Where do you fall on this grid? How can you expand your talents and write essays that create their own definitions?

Memoir

Remember, most essays use elements of different literary approaches. For instance, one piece by John McPhee might contain within it nature writing, science writing, and memoir. But for purposes of scrutinizing our own work and understanding our traditions, we can discuss nonfiction in terms of categories, bearing in mind all the while that we don't want to allow ourselves or the writers we admire to be limited by those categories.

A nonfiction category strongly linked with the personal essay is memoir. *Memoir* comes from the French word for *memory*; no writer of any stripe is prescient enough to put everything he or she wants to record into notes, therefore drawing on memory is an essential part of what we all do. Some readers confuse anything written with a first-person "I" that draws on personal experience with memoir, though new journalists like Joan Didion and Tom Wolfe indulge freely in both without necessarily being memoirists. And some writers, reacting to criticism that the form has become overly confessional and overly prevalent, avoid the term memoir when that's exactly what they're writing.

To be memoir, writing must derive its energy, its narrative drive, from exploration of the past. Its lens may be a lifetime or it may be a few hours. In "Total Eclipse," Annie Dillard recollects a past event, but her narrative drive—the punch of the piece—is metaphysical meditation, not memoir. On the other hand, in his "Afternoon of an American Boy," E. B. White writes a piece of pure memoir. His lens is small; he recalls a period in his teenage years when he first got up the courage to ask a girl out to dance—"that precious, brief moment in life before love's pages, through constant reference, had become dog-eared."

William Zinsser, who edited *Inventing the Truth: The Art and Craft of Memoir*, says, "Unlike autobiography, which moves in a dutiful line from birth to fame, memoir narrows the lens, focusing on a time in the writer's life that was unusually vivid, such as childhood or adolescence, or that was framed by war or travel or public service or some other special circumstance." In other words, memoirists need not have had fascinating lives, worth recounting in every detail. (Those kinds of books, as Zinsser notes, are generally considered autobiography.)

Memoir mines the past, examining it for shape and meaning, in the belief that from that act a larger, communal meaning can emerge. Memoir can heal, it can warn, and it can provide spiritual direction. Spiritual memoir—like the writings of Kathleen Norris and Andre Dubus, among others—falls in the last category. Memoir can open societal lines of communication on subjects previously held taboo. For example, Richard Hoffman's memoir of child sexual abuse, *Half the House*, eventually led to the prosecution of a child molester.

In his essay "Backtalk," Hoffman provides a defense of the surge of memoir as a corrective to a culture that has accepted the verb *to spin* to mean deliberate distortion of our news. "The ascendance of memoir . . . may be a kind of cultural corrective to the sheer amount of fictional distortion that has accumulated in [our] society." For those of you interested in the memoir form,

Hoffman's words may provide a useful starting point; think of yourself as an "unspinner," a voice striving to undo some of the cultural distortion you see around you.

Though memoir is the nonfiction form most closely associated with an "I," it can be written in second or third person; Judith Kitchen uses third person in her brief memoir "Things of This Life," for instance. These kinds of techniques—experiments with point of view, use of different tenses (past, present, future), finding just the right metaphorical image to anchor the piece—all serve to help the memoir elevate itself out of self-centered rumination and into the arena of art.

Literary or New Journalism

In 1972, for an article in *New York* magazine, Tom Wolfe announced "The Birth of the 'New Journalism.'" This new nonfiction form, Wolfe claimed, would supplant the novel. It allowed writers the luxury of a first-person voice and the use of literary devices—scene, imagery, and so forth—in the service of reporting. In other words, Wolfe's new journalism marries traditional journalism with the personal essay. Wolfe cited such new journalists as Hunter S. Thompson, then writing a first-person account of his travels among the Hell's Angels.

Wolfe emerged as one of the leaders of the new journalism, along with other writers such as Joan Didion, Gay Talese, and Norman Mailer. Wolfe rode buses with LSD guru Ken Kesey and his Merry Pranksters to write *The Electric Kool-Aid Acid Test*, all the while using his first-person voice liberally and appearing in his trademark starched high collars and white suits, a character in his own right. Wolfe's insistence on the primacy of his own experience in the act of reporting comes through even in his titles, like this one of an essay about Las Vegas (surely one of the loudest cities in the country): "Las Vegas (What?) Las Vegas (Can't Hear You! Too Noisy) Las Vegas!!!!" New journalism does stress the act of reporting; its practitioners have done some of the most intense reporting in the nonfiction world. But they also avail themselves of literary techniques and a personal voice.

As research becomes more crucial even to very personal nonfiction, such as Terry Tempest Williams's *Refuge* or Andrew Solomon's *The Noonday Demon* (a heavily researched but intimate look at depression), the line between other forms of nonfiction and new journalism blur. And, in the age of instant information on the Internet, traditional journalism becomes more interpretive and less formulaic. Think of it as a healthy blurring of the categories that can sometimes stifle the evolution of forms.

The Meditative Essay

Composing his essays, Montaigne referred to himself as an "accidental philosopher." The term *essay* carries a double meaning of both *trying* and *proving* or *testing*. To essay an action means to attempt it; to essay a substance, particularly a metal, means to test it, weigh it, and try to determine its composition. The essay itself enfolds this dual nature of the term—essays typically approach their subjects tentatively, allow readers the luxury of seeing the author roll ideas around in his or her mind, *test* conclusions rather than presenting them.

The essay form lends itself to tentative, meditative movement, and the meditative essay derives its power from careful deliberation on a subject, often but not always an abstract one. Some meditative essays announce their approach in their title, like Abraham Cowley's *Of Greatness*. In "Total Eclipse," Annie Dillard recalls the event of the eclipse in great detail before switching to her true subject, a metaphysical meditation on our relationship to the universe:

> *The mind wants to live forever, or to learn a very good reason why not. The mind wants the world to return its love, or its awareness; the mind wants to know all the world, and all eternity, and God. The mind's sidekick [the body], however, will settle for two eggs over easy.*

Another example of the meditative essay is Richard Bausch's "So Long Ago." Bausch's meditative intent comes through in the essay's opening, where he addresses the reader in a conversational tone that both engages us and signals that he's about to take us step by step through his thoughts:

Indulge me, a moment.

I have often said glibly that the thing which separates the young from the old is the knowledge of what Time really is; not just how fast, but how illusive and arbitrary and mutable it is. When you are twenty, the idea of twenty years is only barely conceivable, and since that amount of time makes up one's whole life, it seems an enormous thing—a vast, roomy expanse, going on into indefiniteness.

Time—and how we perceive it—is an abstract and slippery subject. Bausch's confiding voice, leading us into his meditation as if we're going into a difficult but rewarding conversation, engages us from the outset. He weaves memories, notably a funeral, among his meditations on the larger importance of time and history. "We come from the chaos of ourselves to the world, and we yearn to know what happened to all the others who came before us. So we impose Time on the flow of events, and call it history."

Without specific events, it's hard to imagine such an abstract meditation holding our interest. The best meditative essayists instinctively make this technique their own. They probe concrete events until they yield up the deeper meanings that lie buried below the surface.

The Sketch or Portrait

One of the most popular essay forms of the nineteenth century, the sketch or portrait held ground partly because of the lack of other forms of communication—the average person traveled little and, even after the invention of photography, saw far fewer photos than we see today. Writers like Dickens stepped into the breach, offering verbal snapshots of cities, foreign countries, and people.

Today we have newspapers, TV, even the Internet, but the power of language to provide not just verbal pictures but emotional ones keeps the portrait an important form. Immediately after the September 11th attacks on the World Trade Center and the Pentagon, the *New Yorker* magazine commissioned a handful of writers to capture that day in short verbal portraits, collectively titled "First Reactions." The editors realized something crucial about that world-changing event: photos may best hold the searing image of the buildings, but a writer can also capture the reality of "stumbling out of the smoke into a different world" (Jonathan Franzen).

The character sketch is also an integral part of the portrait form. Originally a kind of verbal photograph, portraits still can capture individuals in a way visual forms cannot, using imagery and description to leap from someone's surface to their essence. Maxine Hong Kingston's "No Name Woman" forms at once a largely imaginary portrait of the author's disgraced aunt and a portrait of her very real mother:

> *If I want to learn what clothes my aunt wore, whether flashy or ordinary, I would have to begin, "Remember Father's drowned-in-the-well sister?" I cannot ask that. My mother has told me once and for all the useful parts. She will add nothing unless powered by Necessity, a riverbank that guides her life. She plants vegetable gardens rather than lawns; she carries the odd-shaped tomatoes home from the fields and eats food left for the gods.*

What a world of information is packed into this formidable portrait! We see Kingston's mother sketched before us in terms of telling actions—choosing the practical over the ornamental, refusing to waste food, even for presumably religious reasons. We're prepared by this sketch for the tension mother and daughter experience over the suppression of the aunt's story, and the way that story reflects their own uncommunicative relationship.

Humor

Of all the audience responses writers may want to elicit, none is harder to gauge than humor. It's hard to argue about the sentimental value of people falling in love or the tragedy of war, but we all tend to have a comedy vocabulary peculiarly our own. Emily Dickinson, who lends our book its title, had a peculiar habit of roaring with laughter over the obituaries every day. The use of humor in the personal essay dates back to Montaigne and earlier. Let's look at some specifics of what we as a species tend to find funny.

Incongruity

In *How to Write*, Stephen Leacock said, "Humor may be defined as the kindly contemplation of the incongruities of life and the artistic expression thereof." The juxtaposition of odd or unexpected things makes up a lot of what we find comic.

In his essay "The Drama Bug," humorist David Sedaris falls in love with theater and affects a Shakespearean speech that becomes hilarious in juxtaposition with the ordinary events occupying his teenage years. Over a chicken dinner with family, he proclaims, "Methinks, kind sir, most gentle lady, fellow siblings all, that this barnyard fowl be most tasty and succulent." Humor writers like Sedaris are constantly mining their lives for incongruities to use in their work.

The Twist

Like the incongruity, the twist arises from simple surprise—a verbal rug pulled out from under the reader. In *The Deer on a Bicycle: Excursions into the Writing of Humor*, Patrick McManus describes how he fell in love with writing. "I bore down on my next essay with a diligence and concentration previously unknown to me in any academic subject. The effort paid off. A D-minus!"

Given that McManus is detailing the discovery of his vocation, we expect bells to go off with this essay of his—the D-minus comes as a funny (and self-deprecating) surprise. Anne Lamott also offers the reader wonderful twists; hers help ground a spiritual discussion that threatens to become overly solemn. "I believe that every plane I get on is doomed, and this is why I like to travel with Sam [her son]—so that if and when the plane goes down, we will at least be together, and almost certainly get adjoining seats in heaven—ideally, near the desserts."

Life's Irritations

Patrick McManus offers a wonderful piece of advice: write humor out of your bad experiences, not your good ones. Think about it. Which would make a better essay, your best family car trip, with snacks and singing "Kumbaya," or the worst, with your father muttering oaths over a flat tire while your little sister screams for a bathroom or else? What was awful then is probably hilarious now. Some of life's most irritating things—telemarketers, computerized voice answering systems, HMOs—yield some of its most reliable humor.

Exaggeration and Understatement

Exaggeration or hyperbole is a classic American form of humor, dear to practitioners like Mark Twain, who once swore that in a tour of Europe he'd seen the equivalent of a "barrelful" of nails from the True Cross. While the exaggeration is evident, Twain's comment makes a point about the number of false religious relics on display in Europe at the time. Sedaris clearly exaggerates in the long-winded pseudo-Elizabethan speeches he delivers in "The Drama Bug"; no one could remember their own monologues that precisely. (And surely his family would have swatted him with the barnyard fowl before listening to all of that!) Lamott is another comic exaggerator. It's a device she uses again and again to great effect, as when she describes a reading in which "I had jet lag, the self-esteem of a prawn, and to top it off, I had stopped breathing. I sounded just like the English patient."

Self-Deprecation

One characteristic that Sedaris and Lamott have in common is the self-puncturing qualities of the authors. They laugh at themselves so freely we feel encouraged to laugh with them—and, if we're honest with ourselves, we all have a gold mine of material in self-deprecation. No one knows our foibles better than we do. If you look at the Lamott quote—the "self-esteem of a prawn. . . . I sounded just like the English patient"—you'll note that she's laughing above all at how seriously she took herself at the time of this bookstore reading. Most comics exemplify Rodney Dangerfield's "I don't get no respect" attitude. They mine their own insecurities and attempts to make themselves larger—like Sedaris adopting the fake Shakespearean diction—to laugh at themselves and encourage us to laugh at those qualities in them, and in the process, at the whole human condition.

Try It

1. Write a short piece of memoir using a particular event. Write quickly and then examine the piece in light of the distinctions between the intimate and the universal. Where do you speak as though the reader is a friend, listening at your side? Do you need to reveal more of yourself, of your feelings? And where is the universality of your experience? You may want to trade with a partner to uncover the answers to these questions. You can seek out E. B. White's "Afternoon of an American Boy" as a model for this prompt.

> **Variation:** With Richard Hoffman's comments in mind, write a memoir of an event that seeks to "unspin" some kind of official version of it.

2. Write a journalistic story, perhaps about a colorful place nearby or an event in your community (a protest? a festival?) that uses reportorial style to capture the story but also includes your own presence as a character. Use literary devices to describe the people you see; use metaphor to paint their lives. Take advantage of literary devices, while respecting the factuality of journalism.

3. Write a sketch of a person or a place. Focus on keeping your work vivid and simple—a language portrait. Think of it as being intended for someone who cannot meet this person or visit this area.

4. Write an essay titled "On _____." Fill in the blank yourself and use the title as a way to explore an abstract concept in a personal and concrete way. All of us have abstract questions we would secretly love to write about. Why are we here? What does it mean to love a child? Why does society exist in the form it does?

5. Write down the abstract question you would most like to explore. Then freewrite a group of events you somehow associate with that question: a brush with death, giving birth, living in a different culture. Meditate on the question, alternating your meditations with the actual event.

6. Practice writing deliberate incongruities, twists, exaggerations, and understatements. What is the strangest sight you've seen over the last year? Was it a

Hare Krishna at an airport talking on a cell phone? A Santa Claus withdrawing money from an ATM? What experience in your own life led to the most unexpected conclusion, à la McManus's D-minus essay?

7. What irritates you? Write a few paragraphs on the most constant irritants in your life, whether it's telemarketers, the fact that you have almost the same phone number as the local pizzeria, whatever. Write dialogue and scene; strive to be funny. At the same time, think, as previously, of larger subjects this irritant suggests.

8. Actor Billy Bob Thornton constantly pokes fun at himself for his phobias and obsessions, notably a fear of flying and of antique furniture (!). True or not, these self-lampoons are extremely funny. What are your most humorous foibles? What do friends and family lampoon you about? What do these foibles say about you, and our human aspirations?

10

The Lyric Essay

I go out of my way, but rather by license than carelessness. My ideas follow one another, but sometimes it is from a distance, and look at each other, but with a sidelong glance . . . I love the poetic gait, by leaps and gambols.

—MICHEL DE MONTAIGNE

I find myself thumbing through an encyclopedia of Jewish religion I happened to pick up at the library. As I turn the pages of this marvelous book, I'm struck by how little I, a Jewish woman who went to Hebrew school for most of my formative years, know about my own religion. I start writing down the quotes that interest me most, facts about the Kaballah and ritual baths and dybbuks and the Tree of Life. I've also started noodling around with some other stories: a recent trip to Portugal and the news I received there of my mother's emergency hysterectomy; notes on the volunteer work I perform at the local children's hospital; and musings about my on-again, off-again yoga practice. As I keep all these windows open on my computer, the voice of the encyclopedia emerges as an odd, binding thread, holding together these disparate stories in a way that seems organic. I begin to fragment the stories and to move these fragments around, finding the images that resonate against one another in juxtaposition.

I feel like a poet, creating stanzas and listening for the rhythms of the sentence, using white space, reading aloud to determine when another quote from the encyclopedia is necessary to balance out my personal story. Sometimes I have to throw out whole sections that no longer fit, but this editing leaves room for new segments, new phrases, new images that build and transform over the course of the essay, weaving in and out, but always grounded on the thread of prayer and the body. It takes some time, this shuffling gait, but finally I have an essay, "Basha Leah": a spiritual self-portrait in the form of a complex braid.

This lyric essay allows for the moments of pause, the gaps, the silence. The fragmentation feels correct to the piece: it allows for the moments of "not knowing," the unspoken words that seem truer than anything I could ever say aloud.

—BRENDA

What Is the Lyric Essay?

Lyric. Essay. How do these two terms fit together? At first these words may seem diametrically opposed. *Lyric* implies a poetic sensibility concerned more with language, imagery, sound, and rhythm over the more linear demands of narrative. *Essay,* on the other hand, implies a more logical frame of mind, one concerned with a well-wrought story, or a finely tuned argument, over the demands of language. When we put the two together, we come up with a hybrid form that allows for the best of both genres.

To put it simply, lyric essays do not necessarily follow a straight narrative line. The root of the word *lyric* is the lyre, a musical instrument that accompanied ancient song. Lyric poetry and essays are songlike in that they hinge on the inherent rhythms of language and sound. Lyric essays favor fragmentation and imagery; they use white space and juxtaposition as structural elements. They are as attuned to silences as they are to utterance. In its thirtieth anniversary issue devoted to lyric essays, the *Seneca Review* characterized them as having "this built-in mechanism for provoking meditation. They require us to complete their meaning."

The writer of the lyric essay brings the reader into an arena where questions are asked; it is up to the reader to piece together possible answers and interpretations. Fragmentation allows for this type of reader interaction because the writer, by surrendering to the fragmented form, declines a foregone conclusion. Writer and literary theorist Rebecca Faery notes, "In the essays that have in recent years compelled me most, I am summoned, called upon. These essays are choral, polyphonic; there are pauses, rests. . . . The rests in these essays are spaces inviting me in, inviting response."

The lyric essay requires an allegiance to intuition. Because we are no longer tied to a logical, linear narrative or argument, we must surrender to the writing process itself to show us the essay's intent. In so doing, we reveal ourselves in a roundabout way. When we write in the mode of the lyric essay, we create not only prose pieces but a portrait of our subconscious selves, the part of us that speaks in riddles or in brief, imagistic flashes.

Part of the fun of the lyric essay will be making up your own form as you go along. But, for the sake of argument, we will break the lyric essay down into four main categories that seem to encapsulate the lyric essays we see most often: prose poem (or flash nonfiction), collage, the braided essay, and a form we've dubbed the "hermit crab."

Prose Poem or Flash Nonfiction

For the introduction to their anthology *The Party Train: A Collection of North American Prose Poetry*, the editors begin with this piece by S. C. Hahn called "If My Father Were to Ask":

> *"What's a prose poem?" I would turn my face and look into the distance away from our farm house, into a wild copse of trees which runs from the road's edge and on up the hill to the far fields. Box elder, green ash, and black locust tangle in a net of branches, tied together by thorny greenbrier. I know of a coyote den beneath one old box elder tree, on the edge of a gully cutting through the copse. If I were to stick my hand into the hole, I could feel cool wet air and perhaps the playful teeth of pups.*
>
> *"Remember when you plowed the fields in the spring," I say to my father, "and the air behind you filled suddenly with sea gulls?" I can see him inhale the aroma of memory: the green and yellow tractor, the motor exhaust and dust, steel blades of the plow sinking into the earth and turning it, the smell all sexual and holy, worms and grubs uncovered into sunlight, then an unexpected slash of white as the gulls materialize behind the plow, a thousand miles and more from any ocean.*

What is a prose poem? Well, maybe it's the feeling you get when you're standing in a landscape you know well and love, a landscape where you can imagine what lies hidden behind the trees or beneath the ground. Maybe the prose poem is the "aroma of memory" and all the sensual details they evoke. Or maybe the signature of the prose poem is the unexpected surprise at the end, the improbable appearance of sea birds above the plowed fields of the heartland.

Maybe the prose poem is all these things, but most importantly, the prose poem speaks to the heart rather than the head. The prose poem is about what is possible, not necessarily what has already occurred. Even the title, "If My Father Were to Ask," privileges imagination over experience. The father has not asked the question, but what if he did?

In this way, the terms *prose poem* and *flash nonfiction* could be nearly interchangeable. Flash nonfiction is a brief essay—usually less than a thousand words—that focuses on one particular image. It is tightly focused, with no extraneous words, and it mines its central image in ways that create metaphorical significance. The language is fresh, lyrically surprising, hinged on the workings of the imagination. Lawrence Sutin, in his innovative book *A Postcard Memoir*, writes discrete pieces of flash nonfiction as he meditates on the old postcards in his collection. Though the pieces themselves are longer than anything one might write on the back of a postcard, they maintain that same kind of compactness, that intent to be concise and say only what is important for the moment at hand.

This form is fun to both write and read. A new online magazine *Brevity* "publishes concise literary nonfiction of 750 words or less focusing on detail and scene over thought and opinion." W.W. Norton has issued two volumes of short nonfiction, edited by Judith Kitchen and Mary Paumier Jones, called *In Short: A Collection of Brief Creative Nonfiction* and *In Brief: Short Takes on the Personal*. In the introduction to *In Short*, Bernard Cooper elucidates the stance of the lyric essayist working in the flash nonfiction form: "To write short nonfiction requires an alertness to detail, a quickening of the senses, a focusing of the literary lens, so to speak, until one has magnified some small aspect of what it means to be human."

Collage

Do you remember, as a child, making collages out of photographs, images cut from magazines, bits and pieces of text gathered from ticket stubs, documents, or newspaper headlines? Often, these mosaics represented the self in a way that no other form could quite accomplish. Our teachers gazed down at us lovingly as we showed them these renderings, our selves displayed in fragments made beautiful by their juxtapositions.

The collage essay works in the same way. It brings together many different fragments and assembles them so they create something wholly new. *Juxtaposition* becomes the key craft element here. One cannot simply throw these pieces down haphazardly; they must be carefully selected because of how they will resonate off one another. In this way, you act as a painter might, scrutinizing how this particular blue will shimmer against this particular yellow. You must listen for the echoes, the repetitions, the way one image organically suggests the next.

The writer must also provide some kind of grounding structure for the reader to hold onto. Going back to those collages you made as a child, they would be useless collections of fragments without the poster board and glue used to hold the pieces in place. The supporting architecture for a collage essay can take the form of numbered sections, or it can be subtitles that guide the reader along. Or the structure may be as subtle as asterisks delineating the white space between sections. The title, subtitles, or an epigraph (opening quote) can provide a hint of direction for the reader.

For example, in his short essay "My Children Explain the Big Issues," Will Baker relies on the title and the subtitles to hold together four stories about his children he has culled from memory. The subtitles—"Feminism," "Fate," "Existentialism," and "East and West"—do all the explaining he needs to do; they act as bridges, or supports, that allow Baker to write what appear to be four disparate fragments and turn them into one cohesive essay. Without the title or the subtitles, these stories would remain charming vignettes, but they would not carry the impact or hold the focus necessary for an essay. The collage structure works well here because each fragment is allowed to stand on its own while still working in concert with one another. The architecture of the piece works on a subtle level. We think we are reading over the title and subtitles, barely noticing them, but they work on our subconscious throughout our experience of the piece.

Collages work through repetition but not in a monotonous way. You must *transform* your recurring motifs from beginning to end. You must make transitions but not in the conventional way. In the collage essay, transitions occur through the strategic placement of images, stories, and phrases. How does one story lead to the next? Which image can you pick up from the last section to begin the next? Which phrase can act as a repeating and variable mantra throughout the piece? You must trust yourself and your readers to make sense and meaning out of the gaps between steps, the pauses between words, but you must also act as a guide on this pilgrimage, a pathfinder who directs with a touch we barely notice.

The Braided Essay

On the Jewish Sabbath, we eat a bread called challah, a braided egg bread that gleams on its special platter. The braided strands weave in and out of one another, creating a pattern that is both beautiful and appetizing. We eat a special bread on the Sabbath because this day has been set aside as sacred; the smallest acts must be differentiated from everyday motions.

The braided challah is a fitting symbol for an essay form closely allied with collage: the braided essay. In this form, you fragment your piece into separate strands that repeat and continue throughout the essay. There is more of a sense of weaving about it, of interruption and continuation, like the braiding of bread, or of hair.

In his prize-winning essay "After Yitzl," poet Albert Goldbarth braids several different strands together to create a highly textured essay. Written in numbered sections that at first seem to have little to do with one another, the essay works through a steady accretion of imagery and key repetitions; it speaks in a voice that grows loud, then whispers, that cuts itself off, then rambles. The strands include, among other things, a sleepy conversation in bed with a lover, a fabricated "previous life," facts about Mormon religion and Piltdown Man, a story about a cult called the "Unarians," and stories about his own (real) ancestry. The sleepy conversation provides the overall "container" for the essay, an architecture that holds the fragments in place and provides forward momentum to the piece. But by fragmenting this narrative, Goldbarth allows for the other strands to have equal weight. He returns to the conversation over and over and repeats phrases from the other strands, so that the essay never seems to veer off topic.

And that topic slowly reveals itself. The essay turns out to be about how we fabricate our own pasts, constantly and continually; how memory itself is a myth; and how we create ourselves anew in the stories we tell. The braided form allows this theme to emerge organically, to accrue in the reader's mind until it takes on the aspect of an inevitable truth. He explodes his prose to put it together again in a new pattern that is inordinately pleasurable.

The braided form also allows a way for research and outside voices to intertwine with your own voice and experience. When you write a braided essay, find at least one outside voice that will shadow your own; in this way the essay will gain texture and substance.

The "Hermit Crab" Essay

Where we—Suzanne and Brenda—live, in the Pacific Northwest, there's a beautiful place called Deception Pass. Deception Pass is prone to extreme tides, and in the tide pools you can often find hermit crabs skulking about. They look a little like cartoon characters, hiding inside a shell, lifting up that shell to take it with them when they go for cover. They move a few inches, then crouch down and stop, become only a shell again. Then they tilt, waver, and scurry away.

A hermit crab is a strange animal, born without the armor to protect its soft, exposed abdomen. And so it spends its life occupying the empty, often beautiful, shells left behind by snails or other mollusks. It reanimates these shells, making of them a strange, new hybrid creature that has its own particular beauty, its own way of moving through the tide pools and among the rocks. Each one will be slightly different, depending on the type of shell it decides to inhabit.

In honor of these wonderful creatures and the transformative habitat in which they live, we've dubbed a particular form of lyric essay the hermit crab essay. This kind of essay appropriates other forms as an outer covering, to protect its soft, vulnerable underbelly. It is an essay that deals with material that seems born without its own carapace—material that is soft, exposed, and tender, and must look elsewhere to find the form that will best contain it.

The "shells" come where you can find them, anywhere out in the world. They may borrow from fiction and poetry, but they also don't hesitate to armor themselves in more mundane structures, such as the descriptions in a mail-order catalog or the entries in a checkbook register.

For example, in her short story "How to Become a Writer," Lorrie Moore appropriates the form of the how-to article to tell a personal narrative. The voice of the narrator catches the cadence of instructional manuals, but at the same time winks at the reader. Of course these are not impersonal instructions but a way of telling her own story. And by using the literary second person, the reader is unwittingly drawn along into the place of the narrator and a natural interaction develops:

> First, try to be something, anything, else. A movie star/astronaut. A movie star/missionary. A movie star/kindergarten teacher. President of the World. Fail miserably. It is best if you fail at an early age—say, fourteen. Early, critical disillusionment is necessary so that at fifteen you can write long haiku sequences about thwarted desire.

Though "How to Become a Writer" is fiction, the story can act as a fine model for innovative lyric essays in the how-to mode. What are the aspects of your life that you could render in how-to form? How will the second-person address enable you to achieve some distance from the material and thus some perspective? These types of essays can be quite fun to write; the voice takes over and creates its own momentum.

In his essay "Primary Sources," Rick Moody appropriates the form of a foot-noted bibliography to write an autobiography. In "Nine Beginnings," Margaret Atwood takes on two different forms; ostensibly it is a question/answer piece with only one persistent, annoying question. But the title also suggests the form of crumpled first drafts, fished out of the wastebasket. Nancy Willard has written an essay called "The Friendship Tarot" that begins with a sketch of a tarot card layout; she then goes on to insert her autobiographical story into the interpretation of that layout. Several writers have fashioned essays in the form of "to-do" lists. Sei Shonagon has written her lists of "Depressing Things," "Adorable Things," and so forth. The possibilities are endless.

Look around you. The world is brimming with forms that await transformation. A recipe for making soup, handed down by your grandmother, can form the architecture for an essay that fragments a family narrative into the directions for creating something good to eat. An address book that shows the many different places you or your family has lived can begin to shape the material of memory and history. A table of contents, an index, an itinerary, a playlist—all these speak with recognizable voices that might work as the right container for your elusive material.

By taking on the voice of an exterior form for your internal story, you automatically begin the process of creating an artifact out of experience. The form, while it may seem restrictive, actually allows you a great deal of possibility. Suddenly the second-person voice or the third-person perspective is available to you. You're able to take a step back and view your experience through a new lens. Often the form itself will lead to new material you never even suspected.

Think in terms of *transformation*. The word itself means to move across forms, to be changed. Think of the hermit crab and his soft, exposed abdomen. Think of the experiences you have that are too raw, too dangerous to write about. What if you found the right shell, the right armor? How could you be transformed?

TRY IT

1. Go back to one of your own pieces and turn it into fragments. Take a pair of scissors to it and cut it up into at least three different sections. Move these around, eliminating what no longer fits, juxtaposing the different sections in various ways. How can you make use of white space? How can you let the images do the talking for you?

2. Wander the streets of your town looking for random objects. Gather as many of these as you like, then bring them back to your desk and start arranging them in a way that is artistically pleasing. Then write for several minutes on each object and see if you can create a fragmented essay that juxtaposes these elements in the same way.

VARIATION FOR A GROUP: Go out and gather objects individually, but come back together as a group to sift through the pile. Use each other's objects to create three-dimensional collages. Then write for one hour to create a collage essay using these objects as a guide.

3. Write an essay that has fewer than five hundred words. Give yourself a time limit—a half-hour, say—and write about one image that comes to mind or an image that has stayed in your memory from the last couple of days. Use vivid, concrete details. Do not explain the image to us but allow it to evolve into metaphor. If you are stuck, open a book of poetry and write down the first line you see as an epigraph (an opening quote). Write an essay using the epigraph as a starting point for either form or content or imagery. If you write more than five hundred words (about two pages), you must trim and cut to stay under the limit. Find what is essential.

VARIATION FOR A GROUP: Each person should bring in a line of poetry as an epigraph and offer it to a partner. Write for fifteen minutes, and then pass this epigraph to the next person. Write again for fifteen minutes. Continue this process for as long as you like. Try shaping one of these experiments into a complete essay of fewer than five hundred words.

4. Study a painting or a photograph that you have looked at often. What is it about this image that appeals to you so much? Begin a short essay, fewer than a thousand words, that focuses on some unexpected detail that catches your eye in this artwork. Explore this detail for metaphorical significance.

VARIATION FOR A GROUP: Each person brings in a postcard of an artwork; these are all set on a table in the front of the room. Each person browses these postcards and chooses one that appeals to him or her on an intuitive level. Begin writing. You can do this as many times as you like until an image sparks a piece of writing that interests you.

5. Structure an essay around a journey of some sort, using brief, discrete sections to build a collage. This can be a journey to somewhere as commonplace as the mall, or it can be more romantic. What kind of purposeful journey can you imagine taking, such as a pilgrimage to a sacred place?

6. Choose at least three distinctly separate time periods in your life. Begin each section with "I am _____ years old," and freewrite from there. Stay in the present tense. After reading what you've written, see if you can start finding any thematic connections or common images that would link the sections together.

7. Experiment with transitions and juxtaposition. Find one image to repeat in the essay from start to finish, but transform this image in some way so that it has taken on new characteristics by the end of the collage essay.

8. Go back to an essay that's been giving you problems. Look for the one image that seems to encapsulate the abstract ideas or concepts you're trying to develop. Find at least one outside source that will provide new information and details for you. Explode the essay into at least three different strands, each focused on different aspects of that image, and begin weaving.

9. Write an essay in the form of a how-to guide using the second-person voice. You can turn anything into a how-to. In Lorrie Moore's book *Self-Help*, she has stories titled "How to Talk to Your Mother" and "How to Be the Other Woman."

10. Choose a field guide to the natural world as your model ("A Field Guide to Desert Wildflowers," for example, or "A Field Guide to the Atmosphere.") Write an essay in the form of a field guide, inserting your own experience in this format.

11. Write an essay in the form of an interview or as a series of letters.

12. Brainstorm a list of all the forms in the outer world that you could use as a hermit crab essay model. We've done this with groups that have come up with lists of sixty entries and more! The possibilities are endless. Examples of what they came up with include crossword puzzle clues, horoscopes, fortune cookies, letters to the editor, and missing kids flyers. Choose one of these forms and begin an essay, using your own material to flesh out the "shell." Let the word choices and tone of your shell dictate your own approach to your topic. How would the vague cheeriness of fortune-cookie fortunes or horoscopes inform your family or relationship tale?

13. Write a list of the topics/issues in your life that are "forbidden" to speak about, the things you could never write. Choose one of these, and then begin to write about it in a hermit crab form.

11

The Basics of Personal Reportage

Facts in all their glorious complexity make possible creativity. The best nonfiction writers are first-rate reporters, reliable eyewitnesses focused on the world, not themselves, and relentless researchers with the imagination to understand the implications of their discoveries.

—PHILIP GERARD

Working on a book that combined memoir with environmental writing, I found in many areas I was overwhelmed with information. Pesticide research, industrial waste, radiation, and the course of the Cold War: books, papers, old newspapers piled up and slid off my desk, defying all attempts at organization. In other ways, though, I found questions that had no answers: questions about the root causes of environmentally related disease, family stories that were irreconcilably different in everyone's telling. It was an enormous relief to sit at my desk one day and realize that the lack of answers—the evasions, the uncertainties, the whole process—was a story in itself. I continued to research as doggedly as I could, but when I came up blank again and again, I began asking that emptiness whether it had a story to tell. One day I conclude the tale of a particularly frustrating phone call with these words: "I make telephone calls, hour after hour. Mostly I listen to message machines. EPA sends me to DEP, which sends me to ATSDR, which sends me to the County Board of Health, which says it has no records."

By the time I wrote this passage, I had tried to write around what I couldn't uncover, in many awkward and unsuccessful ways. I avoided subjects I needed to confront, or I tried to fake a knowledge I didn't have. I

finally realized—with a liberating shock—that the reader needed to con-
front my own frustrations and uncertainties just as I had, in order to under-
stand this story. The reader needed to hear and see the whole inquiry, even
the phone calls that petered out into more avenues of possibility without
certainty.

—SUZANNE

Cultivating the Need to Know

It should be clear by now that many of the methods we recommend for you to use to expand your subject horizons—placing yourself in history, in the world, braiding, and so forth—are probably going to involve research of some sort or another. Our view of research doesn't mean hours in a library poring over dry technical works, unless that's something you want to do. Anything that takes you out of the realm of what you already know is research. All writers need to expand the ideas that feed them—the "flood subjects," as Emily Dickinson called them—that form those subjects dearest to us for meditation and writing. Our "flood subjects" may never change—if you write about nature, for example, or children, or medicine, you probably always will—but we can and must expand the ground they cover.

Annie Dillard used to teach at our institution, Western Washington University. Science librarians still joke about her weekly forays into the science section and the way she tottered up to the checkout desk with armloads of reference books. Insects, sand, eclipses—nothing escaped Dillard's interest. The range of her interests is evidenced by her essay titles, such as "Death of a Moth" or "Living Like Weasels."

Porosity

Perhaps we can equate openness to research with openness to incorporating the world around us and its events into our own life meditations, a kind of artistic *porosity* to the world around us. Porous materials, such as fabrics, absorb what comes in contact with them. The best nonfiction writers have a special porosity to what is around them; they're unable to ignore even a moth they happen to notice.

Not everyone will want to do full-blown investigative journalism. It's worth remembering that sometimes the best research we can do involves going somewhere we wouldn't normally go and talking to people we wouldn't normally talk to—and of course, really listening. Are you writing an essay about someone who lifts weights? Get a day pass to a gym and absorb the culture of weight-lifting—how lifters push themselves, how muscle curves out of itself when flexed. Imaginatively, see your subject there.

If you want to write about your childhood, don't settle for your memories but look at all the media that shaped your world. Check out magazines from the early years of your life from a library; watch Nickelodeon reruns from that period on television; or go to Historycentral.com and look up the key songs, plays, films, and news events of those years. Confront primary sources, such as documents, photos, films, newspapers, even gravestones; you will often find discrepancies between stories people tell you and the facts you uncover, discrepancies that reveal a lot about your stories and your subjects.

If you are writing about your parents, think about them as human beings at that earlier time—what messages were they hearing? How did those messages help shape them into the people they were?

Using Fact as Metaphor

Factual research will most often be used for what it is: fact. Water may contain a certain complex of chemicals; weight lifting may have such-and-such an effect on the body. These facts can become the basis of an essay that explores the physical wonders and limitations of our world. At times, however, fact will also function as metaphor, informing the essay both on its own terms—information about the physical world the reader may need or find interesting—and as a basis for comparison for a more intangible part of the piece.

One novice writer, Jen Whetham, wrote an essay, "Swimming Pool Hedonist," chronicling how swimming and swimming pools have defined her and held her milestones: learning to trust, early sports success, even a first sexual encounter. The first draft of the essay began by saying "My earliest memory is at a swimming pool," and included a passing reference to the odor of chlorine. That odor turned up again and again, and so Jen researched the chemistry of chlorine; she came up with this section in her final version:

My skin has always smelled like chlorine. . . .

Chlorine is missing one electron from its outer shell: this makes it highly attractive to other molecules. Chlorine's extreme reactivity makes it a powerful disinfectant: it bonds with the outer surfaces of bacteria and viruses and destroys them. When it kills the natural flora on human skin, the reaction creates the stuffy, cloudy smell we associate with chlorine.

Chlorine marks us in ways we cannot see.

The essay goes on to use the touchstone of chlorine—odorless, changing forever what it contacts—as a metaphor for all the invisible ways life touches and changes us, and how we touch and change one another. It is a subtle and nuanced use of fact as fact and fact as metaphor.

Researching a Key Fact or Detail

Peter Balakian set out to write a family memoir in his book *Black Dog of Fate*. Yet, as he probed memories of life with his immigrant family in New Jersey—communal meals, days spent at his grandmother's helping her as she baked—he began to notice that the real story of his family lay in a subject they did *not* discuss: their now-vanished homeland of Armenia, including the fate of family members who had remained there. Finally, by asking questions of his family and doing his own historical research, Balakian came to grips with the real story haunting him: the massacre of the Armenians by the Turks early in the twentieth century. The massacre was so successful it gave Hitler the confidence to conceive of the Holocaust.

In Terry Tempest Williams's "The Clan of One-Breasted Women," the close of her book *Refuge*, Williams begins to examine the larger forces that may be contributing to her family's high breast cancer rate. In the following excerpt, you can see her seamless and organic movement from personal history into researched analysis. She has, as this dialogue begins, told her father of a recurring dream she has of a flash of light in the desert.

"You did see it," he said.

"Saw what?"

"The bomb. The cloud. We were driving home from Riverside, California. You were sitting on Diane's lap. She was pregnant. . . . We pulled over and suddenly, rising from the desert floor, we saw it, clearly, this golden-stemmed cloud, the mushroom. The sky seemed to vibrate with an eerie pink glow. Within a few minutes, a light ash was raining on the car. . . ."

Williams goes on to tell us that "above ground atomic testing in Nevada took place from January 27, 1951, through July 11, 1962." Williams provides an analysis of the political climate of the period—the growth of McCarthyism and the Korean War—summarizes litigation stemming from the tests, and returns seamlessly to her own story. She clearly researches the dates of the bomb testing as well as the wind patterns during those years, but she weaves those facts unobtrusively into her own narrative.

Working with Immersion

Immersion refers to the technique of actually living an experience—usually briefly—to write about it. The late George Plimpton, who was writer and editor of the *Paris Review*, lived for a while as a football player to research the book *Paper Lion*. Lee Gutkind, writer and editor of the journal *Creative Non-fiction*, has done a great deal of immersion writing: he has lived as a circus clown and has followed transplant doctors and umpires on their rounds. Several years ago Robert Sullivan lived for months with the Makah Indian tribe and observed their hunt for gray whales in his book *A Whale Hunt*.

Writers differ in their approaches to immersion research. Gutkind writes of the writer's need to become invisible, almost a piece of furniture in the room with the subject(s): "I like to compare myself to a rather undistinguished and utilitarian end table in a living room or office," he writes. Didion, on the other hand, is always a presence in her research, one whose shy, questioning self forms another character in the piece.

Several years ago a woman we know read about an adult nightclub in Seattle; it was one of the only such clubs in the United States owned and run entirely by women, with a woman-friendly and safe atmosphere. She visited the club, whose dancers were mainly college women and single mothers. Her immersion experience resulted in an essay uncovering a fascinating side of a business generally viewed as exploiting and degrading to women.

Developing Interview Skills

You'll find as many interview styles as there are writers in this world. Writer Gay Talese's polished assurance invites confidence. On the other side of the spectrum are writers like Joan Didion and John McPhee, both of whom describe themselves (or are described by others) as so shy and unsure that interviewees tend to underrate them. It's important to remember artistically as well as ethically that when you conduct research and interview people, their words may ultimately be used in ways they won't like. Didion puts it bluntly, "Writers are always selling somebody out."

Regardless of your style, there are some tips that will help any interview go more productively. Most researchers ask a few "throw-off" questions— those with simple and unimportant answers—to relax their subjects before moving on to more difficult questions. And, as far as that goes, the toughest questions should be saved for last. If someone shuts down because you asked why he or she supported the Iraqi War, for example, you don't want that confrontation to ruin the entire interview. Begin with the simplest and least emotional information, and move forward from there.

Always begin an interview with a list of questions you want to ask; a prepared list will prevent you from forgetting to ask something important because of nerves or simple absentmindedness. Also, end interviews with an open-ended question that will direct you to your next research source. For example, "What do you think is the best place to go for information about the war?" "Are there other people I should speak to about this subject?"

Philip Gerard advises that you always strive to use interviews to find primary sources. "An interview may be a great start," he says, "but will that person also let you read his or her diary, letters, business correspondence?" Gerard tells the story of a F. Scott Fitzgerald scholar who found the most valuable document in studying Fitzgerald turned out to be the writer's tax returns, chronicling his inflated lifestyle and his debt.

Above all, put your questions out there, pause, and really listen. Have your list of questions ready, but be prepared to change course when you get an answer—or a partial answer—that intrigues you. If your subject says casually, "Well, of course John wasn't around then because he was in jail for a while," follow up on that point right away; don't continue with your checklist. You may forget to come back to it, or the person you're speaking to may regret having let it slip. Listen carefully, and follow up on what you hear.

Developing Print Research Skills

Here, we'll explore three commonly used and easily accessed print research sources—the library, the Internet, and primary sources, such as legal documents and statistics.

The Library

The best thing about libraries, we think, is reference librarians. The smallest library contains an overwhelming wealth of information. There are newspapers from all over, going back many years; reference books from the obvious, World Book–type books to dictionaries of chronologies and disasters; specialized encyclopedias; works on microfilm; and tapes and videos. When you know just what you want, the computer or card catalogue will steer you to it. When you don't—say you have a general question about molecular physics or weather or genealogical research—reference librarians will point you to the right sources and help you find what you need.

We went to several of our favorite librarians for advice on how to use the library's resources most effectively. Western Washington University's Paul Piper's first tip was to develop a relationship with your research librarian—introduce yourself, and try to keep working with the same person. He or she will get a sense of what you want and keep a lookout for materials you can use. Piper also recommends spending time articulating to yourself what you're really looking for. He remembers well a patron who asked for books on dogs, then, after wasting quite a bit of time in the dog section, complained she couldn't find anything about the life cycle of the flea there! Dogs are dogs; fleas are fleas. Articulate your interest to yourself as clearly as you can.

Al Cordle, a reference librarian in Portland, Oregon, gave us this piece of advice: "I have a favorite technique for locating books in my library. I always go to the online catalogue and type in one or two keywords to describe my topic and the word *dictionary* or *encyclopedia*. Almost without fail I find specialized reference books devoted to my research topics." Cordle notes that keyword searches, as opposed to subject searches, can be more successful because the search engines operate more flexibly with keywords. Keyword searching should be an option offered by any library computer's toolbar. "So, for example," says Cordle, "if I type *encyclopedia* and *Native Americans*, I may come up with *Encyclopedia of Minorities in American Politics*, *Native Americans: An Encyclopedia of History, Culture, and Peoples*, and *The Encyclopedia of North American Indians*."

Even without the help of a reference librarian, libraries are not hard to navigate if you keep in mind that most print information can be tracked through master sources found in the library's reference section. To begin, articulate to yourself as specifically as you can what information you're looking for. If you had to ask one question to move forward on this writing project, what would it be? Once you have that specific question (or questions) in mind, identify the major reference works that might help you.

If you delve deeply into reference sources covering books and periodical literature, you will come across print sources that sound tantalizingly perfect for your research but that your library does not hold and aren't available on online archives either. Go to the information desk and inquire about your library's interlibrary loan policy. Almost anything, including out-of-print books and old newspapers on microfilm, can be borrowed through interlibrary loan. You may have to wait a few weeks for the text to appear and do a lot of reading rather quickly once it arrives, as these items generally can only be kept for several weeks. But knowing you've solved a puzzle or put together information no one else has by tracking little-known sources is part of the thrill of research.

The Internet

Most researchers agree the Internet forms the most important new research tool we have now, offering access to trillions of pages of material at the touch of a finger. This massive access also forms the Internet's biggest drawback: the large volume of unsorted material it turns up. Still, it's one of the best quick sources of information available now, especially for facts that don't hold too much ambiguity. If you want to know the migration habits of the gray whale, a quick search will get this information for you, along with maps and sound (if your computer has speakers) that will enable you to hear the grays making their way along the coast. This is quite a large payoff for very little effort.

Reva Basch, coauthor of *Researching Online for Dummies*, breaks down the areas in which Internet research is most useful. The first is to get background information on a subject, and the second is for fact-checking. AskJeeves and Refdesk.com are both highly recommended sites for fact-checking, and a site like the Library of Congress's American Memory (memory.loc.gov/ammem /amhome.html) will give you an excellent overview of any subject that could be considered historical, such as Watergate, or more recent topics like the last election. American Memory, like many other resource sites, even houses video and audio clips.

A number of search engines track what's published in thousands of print sources, and many offer abstracts or summaries of the articles— some offer complete copies. Check your library for its list of online resources to see what specialized search engines you can use there if the right engines aren't available on your home computer (assuming you have one). A few to look for: Infotrak, which is an exhaustive list of periodical publications; PDQ, which offers in many cases abstracts and complete articles; and Northern Light's Special Collections (northernlight.com), which gives access to many specialized magazines. (Northern Light charges a small fee, but your library may offer it for free.)

If you can think of an institution that would house information you need, consider checking its website. Museums, government organizations, the Library of Congress, all offer immense amounts of information on the Web. You might, for instance, wonder what the Smithsonian Institution in Washington, D.C., a premier science source, could tell you about eclipses. Use a search engine to access the Smithsonian's site, then follow its navigation instructions to access its online resources. You can often figure out Web addresses even without search engines; if you want information on nuclear energy, you might start with the U.S. Department of Energy. Put their abbreviation (DOE), with the .gov suffix used by all government agencies, after the basic World Wide Web address of www, and voila—there it is.

There are services available on the Web, called research services, that find articles for free and then make money by charging you for copies. One that uses a powerful search engine and does not require an initial fee, recommended by *Rules of Thumb for Research*, is Colorado Alliance of Research Libraries (CARL) at carl.org. If you find a helpful-looking article, you can either pay the small fee charged by CARL for a copy, or try to find the article through a local library.

You can begin playing with Internet research—assuming you haven't done this already—by choosing a good browser and search engine and typing in key words or phrases that capture your interest. Give this process a dry run just to see how it feels—choose a subject that has either interested you for a long time, or something you take absolutely for granted, maybe "the molecular structure of DNA" or "the electoral college." (We don't think much of the vagaries of how we vote, we just do it.)

Learn to scrutinize both the search engine summaries and the sites themselves for clues to how useful or downright flaky they are. The suffixes .edu and .gov, for instance, indicate sites run by educational institutions (edu) and the U.S. government (gov). A number of sites run by leading-edge universities like MIT have pages on the molecular structure of DNA, as does the World Book online (worldbookonline.com); the identities of these sources are clear from their URLs, or Web addresses. Several government sites, denoted by their .gov suffix, have good explanations of the electoral college. Lots of sites will also come up that you'll probably want to give a pass—sites not relevant to your question, personal online diaries, even stories about alien DNA! Or maybe these are another essay altogether.

Remember that computers are literal creatures. The woman searching for information on fleas can stumble through an explanation by looking for dog books, however much time she may lose approaching the subject that way. No search engine, however, can intuit the leap from "dog" to "flea." Phrase your search as precisely as you can without narrowing it down too much. "AIDS in Africa" will result in hundreds of thousands of sites; "AIDS in unwed mothers between the ages of twenty-eight and twenty in the lower Volta delta" probably won't yield any. And try alternative terms to see if you uncover more or better results—both "FBI" and "Federal Bureau of Investigation," for example.

Primary Sources

One writer we know wanted to research a point in family history about which he'd heard conflicting stories—his grandparents' marriage and the birth of his mother. Visiting the courthouse in the county where the marriage took place, he requested his grandmother's marriage license and was handed a license to a marriage other than the one to his grandfather. Intrigued, he recovered copies of both marriage licenses, wedding announcements that ran in the newspapers of the time, and his mother's birth certificate—and discovered his grandmother had been pregnant and just divorcing when she married his grandfather. Back in the 1930s both events would have prompted a great deal of scandal. Tensions in family relationships suddenly fell into place.

You may not discover anything quite so interesting, or you may find something far more interesting, but the fact is, courthouses keep records of births, adoptions, marriages, divorces, deaths, and more. Anyone can request copies; you visit the courthouse in the proper town or county, ask to see the directory of records, and request copies of what you want. Or you register with an online service like Courtlink (lexisnexis.com/courtlink), which, for a fairly low fee, can generally obtain legal documents on file anywhere in the country. If you're researching a topic in a particular town, you might want to try the historical society; most towns have them, and they keep all sorts of documents, including deeds of sale, photographs, and frequently, diaries and old publications. Old newspapers, too, teem with information, and are kept in local libraries on microfilm. You may want to back up your family interviews with research into what really happened.

There are so many other print sources of information they're hard to list here. The Government Printing Office, for example, has reports and statistics available on everything imaginable, from Congressional testimony to government-sponsored research. The Television Archives housed at Vanderbilt University contain tapes of television broadcasts, including news broadcasts as well as programs, going back to the earliest days of television. You can also request written transcripts of old broadcasts. It's possible, through intelligent research, to immerse yourself completely in another place and time.

Winnowing Down

Here's an example of the genesis of a research-driven essay. Jennifer Price, author of the essay "A Brief Natural History of the Plastic Pink Flamingo," commented that she had "no desire to write about the flamingo until I learned the guy who invented it was named Featherstone, he and his wife wore matching outfits every day that his wife sewed, and they had a poodle named Bourgeois." These stray facts convinced Price the lawn flamingo, brainchild of an eccentric inventor, might hold a story she wanted to tell.

In the course of investigating the American phenomenon of lawn flamingos, Price learned that people from film directors to *New Yorker* editors held cherished collections of the birds, and that one lawn flamingo had been kidnapped; its kidnappers sent back photographs "from" the bird as it traveled the world, against backdrops like the Eiffel Tower in Paris. "I couldn't believe one lawn ornament could represent so much," said Price, who stumbled into this story through a casual bit of research.

From those beginnings, where we fall in love with a piece of information, essays begin; the shaping that follows, however, can be difficult. At this early stage of research, Jennifer Price had to ask herself which story she really wanted to tell, Featherstone's or the flamingo's. (As the essay title indicates, she chose the latter.) The toughest thing about research is learning to sort through what you find, particularly now, in the midst of the Internet explosion and the Information Age. Imagine you're Jennifer Price, feeling just a tickle of interest in writing an essay about pink plastic lawn flamingos. A search on a powerful search engine—google.com—takes several seconds and unearths almost three hundred sites, each one loaded with lawn flamingo information.

Without looking any further, you can scan the search engine summaries and learn all these facts: lawn flamingos were initially designed using photographs from *National Geographic*, they've stirred up dissent when used to create Nativity scenes at Christmas, and the creator of them got an award from the satirical *Journal of Irreproducible Results*. This quick scan creates practically an essay in itself, without bothering to click on the sites and learn even more.

What do you do with it all? First of all, keep close to you the initial impulse that made you want to do this research—the first fact or hint that gave you a sense you had a subject for an essay you could live with, even grow obsessive about, for a while. It's important to avoid the temptation to drop into your essay everything you learn that's strange or amusing. Jennifer Price began her essay with an interest in flamingo creator Don Featherstone, but she found, sorting through her material, that it was the flamingos' borderline between artifice and nature that captured her.

What is closest to your own heart, your own obsessions? What in this research do you feel most qualified and eager to talk about? Sit with your papers, including interview notes, in front of you, and circle or highlight the material that feels most to draw you or belong to you. You can try making piles in order of urgency: what you must write about, what you probably should include, what's more iffy.

Once you've done some basic highlighting and sorting, if you are working on a piece with a great deal of research—not just a key fact, like the eclipse shadow—it helps to create a computer file or notebook page with a list of material you want to use. Put facts in an order that feels like it might correspond to the order you'll use them in, but don't burden yourself by treating this as an outline. Your writing should always stay fluid, flexible, and open to your best intuitive leaps. Consult the list as you draft, to see if there are any exciting facts—those that help explain, that offer metaphorical possibilities, and so forth—which you've forgotten.

Try It

1. Pull out an essay you've been working on, one that has promise but doesn't feel quite finished yet. Make a list of facts that inform this piece—none of these facts needs to be present in the work but implied, either through location, time, action, or characters. Here's a sample opening paragraph, and the list it generates.

It is 1963 and I am watching, for what seems like the hundredth time,
Lee Harvey Oswald collapse as he is shot by Jack Ruby. I am wearing my
Winnie the Pooh pajamas and listening to the ice clink in my mother's
glass as she drinks another gin in the kitchen. I've told her I'm watching
"Rocky & Bullwinkle" but by this time of night she's too far gone to pay
attention.

This is a very promising start: emotional without any trace of self-indulgence, nicely detailed. Here's a list of possible research areas:

- Kennedy assassination: political climate of the time? Bay of Pigs?
- Media in the early 1960s
- Post-war Midwest (unstated in the opening, but this is the location)
- Alcoholism, particularly during this period. What was the medical view of alcoholism? The social view? How was alcohol portrayed in the media of the time?

Going down the list, the author decides that alcoholism is the most promising avenue for further study. She begins by looking at advertisements and films from the period, seeing how alcohol is portrayed: as an everyday diversion, the province of sophisticates and James Bond–types. She explores medical textbooks dating from the 1960s to probe how alcohol dependence was viewed then. She finds it a much more character-driven view, less a disease model, than today. Finally, she browses Alcoholics Anonymous literature to see how a sense of the disease of alcoholism has evolved.

The final step is highlighting information worth using and then working it into the author's story without a change of voice: it's important not to sound textbook-y, as if another author has come in to serve as newscaster. Compare two moves this author could make next, given below:

In 1963, more than half of Americans, current experts agree, use alco-
hol to excess, and 75 percent of films show characters drinking alcoholic
drinks.

Or:

Everybody is in love with James Bond this year, who drinks martini after
martini in his movies without any change in behavior. James Bond has

made "shaken, not stirred" a mantra for this martini-smitten culture.
My mother simply eliminates the vermouth.

2. The next time a strange fact grabs your attention write it down or, if it appears in a newspaper or magazine, cut out the source. Ask yourself why this fact seems to demand your attention. Write an essay based on this fact, using additional research if necessary. If you're trolling for odd facts, try almanacs or *Harper's Index*, which holds a plethora of bizarre tidbits, like the fact that the Pentagon spends $100 a minute on Viagra.

3. Chances are you've already had at least one terrific immersion experience, even if you didn't call it that: maybe it was the wedding you attended where the bride and groom were Goths who married in black robes with white talcum on their faces. Maybe it was the time your uncle dragged you along to a meeting of the local Elks Club. Fascinating immersion experiences exist all over. Do you live near a hospital? A casino? A group of Wiccans? A Society for Creative Anachronism? Ask them if they would mind you observing them a while for an essay. Keep notes, use a tape recorder, or both.

Decide, before you begin your immersion experience, how you see your role. Will you take the approach of Didion and acknowledge your presence in the events you write about, or, like Gutkind, try to keep yourself out of the narrative? Adjust your presence accordingly.

4. To hone your interview skills and create a body of information you'll almost certainly want to come back to, try family interviews. These interviews are generally far less intimidating than tracking down your local physicist to ask questions about the implications of the Big Bang. Families also tend to be repositories of fascinating hidden information—uncles who had more money than they should have, cousins who disappeared in disgrace.

Start with a question you have always wanted to get an answer—or a clearer answer—to. It may be the life story of the family scapegrace, an immigration story, or a detailed picture of a parent's early years. Make a list of questions; keep them fairly simple. If you're pursuing the story of a family member in legal trouble, your questions might include what year that trouble first occurred, full details of it, how family members responded, and so forth.

Ask your questions of two or three different family members—preferably including several generations, such as a cousin, a parent, a grandparent—and make note of the discrepancies between their versions of events. Unless your family is very different from most, there will be plenty. Follow up on your initial interviews with further questions, to see if you can explain differing versions of the story.

This second round of questions will tell you a lot about the person/event you're researching, and it will also tell you a lot—maybe even more—about the structure of your family. Typically, families have keepers-of-the-family-name types, who minimize or dismiss what seems "improper." They also have tell-all types—those who collect stories and relish relating them. You may want to meditate on who plays these roles in your family (does the answer surprise you?) and, of course, who you are in the hierarchy of things.

PART 3

HONING YOUR CRAFT

Let men and women make good sentences. Let them learn to spell the sound of the waterfall and the noise of the bathwater. Let us get down the colors of the baseball gloves, the difference in shade between the centerfielder's deep pocket and the discreet indentation of the catcher's mitt. . . . Let us enlist the Vocabulary, the Syntax, the high grammar of the mysterious world.

—STANLEY ELKIN

12

The Basics of Good Writing
in Any Form

I was delighted to find that nonfiction prose can also carry meaning
in its structures and, like poetry, can tolerate all sorts of figurative
language, as well as alliteration and even rhyme. The range of
rhythms in prose is larger and grander than it is in poetry, and it can
handle discursive ideas and plain information as well as character and
story. It can do everything. I felt as though I had switched from a
single reed instrument to a full orchestra.

—ANNIE DILLARD

People need maps to your dreams.

ALLEN GURGANUS

*I am working with a group of novice nonfiction writers, and we're about
two-thirds of the way through our time together. My students have plumbed
their lives in ways they never thought possible: as environmental records, as
living history, as a movement through various forms—scientific, spiritual,
cultural, aesthetic—of inquiry. They sort themselves through the door of my
classroom with varying degrees of eagerness, and pull out their notebooks,
pens cocked and waiting. They're used to coming in and interrogating themselves in different ways: Who are they really? How have they lived? Today,
however, I know I'm going to make them groan. Instead of prompts like
writing about the explosion of Mount St. Helens or the World Trade Orga-*

nization riots in Seattle, I have them pull out a piece of their own prose and count the number of words in each sentence for three paragraphs. I also have them jot down comments on the kinds of sentences they use: simple declarative (basic subject-verb), complex, fragmented, and so forth. They do the assignment, because it would be even more boring to sit and do nothing, I suppose. Suddenly a little exclamation breaks out from a corner of the room.

"Ohmigod!" says one young woman. "All of my sentences are eleven words long!"

This young woman has been concerned about what feels to her like a flatness or lifelessness to her prose. Here, in one rather mechanical but not painful exercise, she's put her finger on the reason, or one of the reasons. On further analysis she discovers that she has a penchant for writing one simple declarative sentence after another: "I drive to the forest in April. My car is almost ready for a new clutch. The forests are quiet at that time of year." The metronomic beat of same sentence structure, same sentence length, has robbed her otherwise sparkling essays of their life.

For the sake of comparison, listen to the difference created in those three sample sentences by a little more rhetorical inventiveness: "In April, a quiet time of year, I drive to the forest. My car almost ready for a new clutch."

—SUZANNE

Scene Versus Exposition

Generally speaking, scene is the building block of creative nonfiction. There are exceptions to this statement—more academic or technically oriented writing, the essay of ideas perhaps—but overall, the widespread notion that nonfiction is the writer's thoughts presented in an expository or summarizing way has done little but produce quantities of unreadable nonfiction. Scene is based on action unreeling before us, as it would in a film, and it will draw on the same techniques as fiction—dialogue, description, point of view, specificity, concrete detail. Scene also encompasses the lyricism and imagery of great poetry. We have, as the Dillard quote at the head of this chapter indicates, access to the full orchestra. We need to learn to play every instrument with brio.

Let's begin by defining our terms. *Expository* writing, as the term implies, exposes the author's thoughts or experiences for the reader; it summarizes, generally with little or no sensory detail. Expository writing compresses time: *For five years I lived in Alaska.* It presents a compact summation of an experience with no effort to re-create the experience for the person reading.

On the other hand, *scene*, as in fiction, uses detail and sensory information to re-create experience, generally with location, action, a sense of movement through time, and possible dialogue. Scene is cinematic. Here is a possible reworking of the above sentence, using scene: *For the five years I lived in Alaska I awoke each morning to the freezing seat of the outhouse, the sting of hot strong coffee drunk without precious sugar or milk, the ringing "G'day!" of my Australian neighbor.*

The latter version of this sentence clearly presents the reader with a more experiential version of that time in Alaska, with details that provide a snapshot of the place: the slowness of time passing is stressed by the harsh routine of the coffee and outhouse; we get a sense of scarcity of supply; the neighbor even has a bit of swift characterization. Of course, for an essay in which Alaska is totally unimportant the expository summation might be the better move. But if you find yourself writing nonfiction with very little scene, you are likely to produce flat writing readers have to struggle to enter.

Remember "The Knife," by author/surgeon Richard Selzer? This essay moves fluidly between scene and exposition; Selzer forces us to *live* the awesome power and responsibility of the surgeon before allowing himself the luxury of meditating about it.

> *There is a hush in the room. Speech stops. The hands of the others, assistants and nurses, are still. Only the voice of the patient's respiration remains. It is the rhythm of a quiet sea, the sound of waiting. Then you speak, slowly, the terse entries of a Himalayan climber reporting back. "The stomach is okay. Greater curvature clean. No sign of ulcer. Pylorus, duodenum fine. Now comes the gall-bladder. No stones. Right kidney, left, all right. Liver . . . uh-oh."*

Selzer goes on to tell us he finds three large tumors in the liver. "Three big hard ones in the left lobe, one on the right. Metastatic deposits. Bad, bad."

Like fine fiction, this passage contains a clear setting—the hospital room, characterized appropriately enough by sound rather than appearance: the silence of life and death. There is action mimicking real time, containing the element of surprise. We learn along with the surgeon about the patient's metastasized cancer. There's dialogue, as the surgeon narrates to himself, to his surgical assistants, seemingly to the fates, his discovery of the patient's mortality. And, like fine poetry, this piece of writing also organizes itself through imagery: the "quiet sea" of the passive patient's breathing versus the labored voice—like a "Himalayan climber's"—of the surgeon emphasizes the former's loss of control.

Selzer's passage would be easy to change to an expository sentence: *Often in surgery I found unexpected cancer.* But the author's final purpose—an extended meditation on the relationship of human and tool, soul and body—would fall flat. The reader, lacking any feel for the grandeur and potential tragedy of exploring the body, would dismiss expository statements such as, "The surgeon struggles not to feel. It is suffocating to press the feeling out," as merely odd or grandiose.

There are several other moves worth noting in this passage. One is that, like the sample Alaska sentence given above, Selzer's surgical description is *representative scene.* In other words, he doesn't pretend this operation occurs at one specific time and place, but it represents a typical surgical procedure, one among many. Another technique to note is his use of the second person for a speaker that is presumably himself. Second person—the *you* rather than the *I*—is a point-of-view choice, discussed in more detail further on in this chapter.

In contrast, here's an example of a specific, not representative, scene, from Jo Ann Beard's essay "The Fourth State of Matter." The scenes comprising the essay all occur at very specific moments in time. Here is Beard at work, with her physicist colleagues having a professional discussion around the chalkboard:

> "If it's plasma, make it in red," I suggest helpfully. We're all smoking illegally, in the journal office with the door closed and the window open. We're having a plasma party.
>
> "We aren't discussing plasma," Bob says condescendingly. He's smoking a horrendously smelly pipe. The longer he stays in here the more it feels like I'm breathing small daggers in through my nose. He and I don't get along;

each of us thinks the other needs to be taken down a peg. Once we had a
hissing match in the hallway which ended with him suggesting that I could
be fired, which drove me to tell him he was already *fired, and both of us*
stomped into our offices and slammed our doors.
  "I had to fire Bob," I tell Chris later.
  "I heard," he says noncommittally. Bob is his best friend.

This is a very pinpointed event, not representative but presumably unlike any other moment in Beard's life. Notice how much suggestive detail Beard packs into a short space. These characters break rules, argue, and exist in complex relationship to one another. Her relationship with Bob is established in this scene—a relationship that seems suffused with a genuine but relatively harmless tension, given their ability to issue dire threats to each other without consequence. The dialogue sounds real and secures the characters, capturing the nuanced pretense of Bob's stressing the "plas" part of the "plasma." Chris, the man in the middle, seems to have heard all this bickering before.

We all tend to use too little scene in creative nonfiction. We especially forget the possibilities of representative scene. Even when we're reporting a typical rather than a specific event, use of scenic elements, as in Selzer's surgery, conveys a sense of character and situation far more effectively than does summary.

Specificity and Detail

Scene forces us to use specificity and detail, elements that get lost in the quick wash of exposition. Even in discussing the largest ideas, our brains engage with the small workings of the senses first. And the specificity of a piece of nonfiction is generally where the sensory details lie: the aroma of honeysuckle, the weak film of moonlight. While it is possible to go overboard with detail, generally in drafting it's best to keep going back and sharpening as much as possible. You leaned not just against a tree but against a weeping silver birch; the voice at the other end of the phone sounded like the Tin Man's in *The Wizard of Oz*. Your readers or writing group can tell you when you've gone too far. When you write scene, your job is to mimic the event, create an experiential representation of it for the reader.

Look at the examples given before, and think about how much the details add to those scenes: the hushed silence of the hospital room and three hard tumors on the right lobe of the liver in Selzer's essay. In Beard's, we see the bickering but ultimate acceptance of this close group of coworkers. We sense the author's ambivalent position in the group—shut out of their "talking physics," as she tells us earlier—but also her authority within the group. We sense, in the hyperbolic description of Bob's pipe smoke ("like daggers"), a bit of foreshadowing of a coming tragic event.

In *The Elements of Style*, William Strunk, Jr., explains that the one point of accord among good writers is the need for detail that is "specific, definite, and concrete." (We also address this point in Chapter 1.) Concrete detail appeals to the senses; other writers call such details "proofs." If Selzer told us readers that sometimes in surgery he found cancer, we might abstractly believe him, but it's hard to associate that fact with real life and death. In this passage, we're convinced by the specifics: three hard tumors on the liver, the surgeon's voice mumbling, "Bad, bad."

Abstract language—the opposite of relying on concrete detail—refers to the larger concepts we use that exist on a purely mental level, with no appeal to the senses: *liberty*, *justice*, *contentment*, and so on. These terms may contain the implication of sensory detail (you may flash on "warmth" when you hear "contentment," but that's a personal reaction that wouldn't make sense to, say, a penguin), but they are in themselves broad categories only. Of course, within the details you use emerges a wealth of abstract information. Beard could have summarized her relationships with her coworkers; Selzer could have presented a few expository sentences about soul and body, surgeon as God. We want experiences, not lectures; we want to enter into events and uncover their meanings for ourselves.

Paying attention to concrete detail and the input of our own senses also helps save us from the literary pitfall of cliché, an expression or concept that's been overused. Frequently, clichés are dead metaphors, so overused we don't pay attention anymore to the comparisons they contain. (Do you actually think of a yellow metal when you hear "good as gold"? Do you even realize this phrase comes from a time when the gold our country held validated our money?) If Beard had described Bob's pipe tobacco as smelling like "dirty socks," or "killing" her nose, she would have been indulging in cliché. Instead, she used the information of her senses to create a fresh image.

Chances are, you know more than you need to know to write effective scene, but your natural expressiveness has been stifled, often by misguided advice from academic writing classes. Next time you work on a piece of creative nonfiction, hear yourself talking through the story to friends in a crowded coffee shop or club. There's plenty to divert their attention: music, people-watching, smoke, and noise. Which details do you use to hold their attention? Do you imitate the look of someone's face, the sound of a voice? Do you screech to demonstrate the sound of car tires on asphalt? Your reading audience will be equally distractible. Think about how to render these attention-grabbing devices in your prose. You may want to consult Chapter 1, "The Body of Memory," to remind yourself how to use sensory detail.

Developing Character

Character development, like learning to write effective dialogue, is part of writing scene. It's another particularly easy-to-miss demand of good creative nonfiction. After all, *we* know what our parents, children, or lovers look like. Unconsciously, we tend to assume that everyone else does as well.

Suzanne has, by marriage, a very funny grandmother. She wasn't intentionally funny, but nonetheless the mere mention of her name tends to bring down the room when the family's together. The family bears in mind, as courteous people, that we need to break through our uncontrollable giggling and clue other listeners in to the source of our amusement: "Well, she came from a tiny town in south Georgia and talked about nothing all day long but her ar-ther-itis and her gallbladder that was *leakin'* plus she lied compulsively and pursed her mouth in this funny way when she did. . . ." After a few minutes of this our auditors understand why we find her so endlessly amusing. This kind of filling in, also natural in conversation, is the essence of character development.

Nothing demonstrates the power of fine characterization like studying writers who, in a few strokes, can help us apprehend someone sensually (through sight, sound, or feel) as well as give us a sense of their essence. The following are examples of quick, effective character development from essays we love:

- **Albert Goldbarth in "After Yitzl":** "My best friend there shoed horses. He had ribs like barrel staves, his sweat was miniature glass pears."
- **Lawrence Sutin in "Man and Boy":** "In the case of my father and myself, I had the fullness of his face and his desire to write, which had been abandoned when he came to America with a family to raise. . . . He was a middle-aged man who was sobbing and sweaty and his body was heavy and so soft I imagined his ribs giving way like a snowman's on the first warm winter day."
- **Judith Kitchen in "Things of This Life":** "Mayme would step onto the platform wearing a dark purple coat, her black braids wound tightly around her head. Her skin was too soft and wrinkly. When you kissed her cheek, it wobbled, and you wished you didn't have to do that."

Details that give a sense of the essence of an individual—in all his or her typicality (commonness with their type; grandmothers typically have soft and wrinkly skin) and individual, specific glory (sweat like miniature pears)—are hard to define, but blazingly effective when you come upon them. Think, when you write about someone close to you, how you would characterize that person in a stroke or two for someone else.

Dialogue

It can be difficult to allow ourselves to use direct dialogue in creative nonfiction. After all, memory's faulty; we can't recall conversations word for word, so why try? The answer is that we need to try, because insofar as nonfiction attempts to be an honest record of the observant mind, dialogue matters. We recall voices, not summaries; we observe scenes in our head, not expository paragraphs.

Dialogue generally moves action forward. Selzer quotes himself finding the metastasized cancer, and Beard gives a sense of the dynamics of her office. Dialogue must characterize and capture the voice of the speaker, however, not simply give information. The latter is called in fiction writing "information dumping," and it occurs when you have people say things like, "Well, Carmen, I remember you told me you were taking the cross-town bus that day only because your white 1999 Volvo had developed a gasket problem." Information dumping is less of a problem in nonfiction because this genre is reality based (and people really *do not* talk that way). But, if you cue your readers that you are re-creating a conversation, it may be tempting to lard the dialogue with information you can't figure out how to get in any other way. Don't do it.

Everyone has a natural cadence and a dialect to his or her speech. We nearly always speak in simple sentences, not complex-compound ones. We might say, "When the rain comes, the grass grows," which has one short dependent clause beginning with the word "when"; we aren't likely to say, "Whenever it happens the rain comes, provided the proper fertilizer's been applied, grass grows, unless it's been masticated by cows grazing thereon"—a simple sentence or *main clause* ("the grass grows") festooned with wordy subordinate clauses. We frequently speak in sentence fragments or ungrammatical snippets—e.g., the how-are-you question "Getting along?" instead of the grammatically correct "Are you getting along?" One exception to these rules of natural speech might be a person who *is* pompous and wordy. Perhaps you're writing dialogue to capture the voice of a stuffy English professor you know. In that case, go to town. Just bear in mind that what bores you will bore others fairly quickly. In the case of people who are boorish, dull, or otherwise hard to listen to, give readers a sample of the voice and they will fill in the rest. A little goes a long way.

One final caveat: beware of elaborate taglines, which identify the speaker, such as "he said," "she argued," and so forth. In dialogue between two people taglines are often dispensable after the first two. Even when you must use them, stick as much as possible to "said" and "asked," two fairly invisible words in the context of dialogue. It's an easy mistake to make—and a difficult one to overlook as a reader—to have all of your characters "retort," "storm," or "muse." And make sure the words themselves contain tone as much as possible. (Tone can also be conveyed in a character's gesture, as in Beard's colleagues casually breaking the rules by smoking in their office.) Don't follow each speech tag with an adverb such as "angrily," "sadly," and so on. If you feel the need to use those words, ask yourself why the dialogue itself doesn't seem to contain those feelings.

Point of View

Every story is told by a storyteller (even in a piece with multiple speakers, one speaker dominates at a time), and every storyteller must be situated somehow within the frame of the work. This situating is called *point of view* (POV), and we express it through choice of pronouns. To put it simply, the tale can be told by an "I" (first-person POV), a "you" (second person), or a "he" or "she" (third person). Though it may seem at first blush as though all nonfiction must be told in first person, skillful writers do use the techniques of second- and third-person POV to wonderful effect in nonfiction. And the more the genre stretches its limbs, takes risks, and remakes its rules, the more such untraditional devices appear, and the more aware we become as writers of what they can do.

Of the three point-of-view choices, second person is the rarest, in nonfiction as well as in fiction and poetry. It's not hard to figure out why: second-person POV calls attention to itself and tends to invite reader resistance. Imagine recasting "For five years I lived in Alaska" as "For five years you lived in Alaska." That's exactly what a POV shift to second person would do; it places the reader directly in the shoes of the author, without narrative mediation. Clumsily used, second person screams out for the reader to say, "No, I didn't" with an inner shrug of indignation and stop reading. Skillfully used, however, that blurring of line between reader and author can be very powerful.

Here's a sentence from "The Fourth State of Matter" again, a classic first-person approach: "It's November 1, 1991, the last day of the first part of my life." Compare that with a short passage from Richard Selzer, who uses second person liberally throughout his essay. Watch the careful way he slips from first- to second-person POV, as if inviting the reader to experience the fearfulness of a surgeon's power:

> *I must confess that the priestliness of my profession has ever been impressed on me. In the beginning there are vows. . . . And if the surgeon is like a poet, then the scars you have made on countless bodies are like verses into the fashioning of which you have poured your soul.*

In contrast, Judith Kitchen's essay "Things of This Life" uses third person throughout the piece to create a sense of freshness and excitement in a childhood memoir:

> *Consider the child idly browsing in the curio shop. She's been on vacation in the Adirondacks, and her family has (over the past week) canoed the width of the lake and up a small, meandering river. . . . So why, as she sifts through boxes of fake arrowheads made into key chains, passes down the long rows of rubber tomahawks, dyed rabbits' feet, salt shakers with the words "Indian Lake" painted in gold, beaded moccasins made of what could only in the imagination be called leather, is she happier than any time during the past week?*

Kitchen, further along in the essay, tells us, "Now consider the woman who was that child." It seems at first an odd choice, to write about the self as if it were someone completely apart, a stranger. But as Kitchen unfolds her sense of her life as "alien," a space she's inhabiting that raises questions she still can't answer ("How can she go on, wanting like this, for the rest of her life?"), the strategy becomes a coherent part of the architecture of the essay.

Imagine the paragraphs it would take to explain such an alienation from the self—a sense of distance from one's own desires—and the relative powerlessness such an explanation would have. Annie Dillard writes in our introductory quote that she "delighted" to learn that nonfiction, like poetry, can carry meaning in its structures. Kitchen here has wisely chosen a structure to convey her feeling—a feeling open only to the clumsiest articulation.

Image and Metaphor

Janet Burroway, in her text *Writing Fiction*, describes metaphor as the foundation stone "from which literature derives." Image—any literary element that creates a sense impression in the mind—and metaphor—the use of comparison—form the heart of any literary work. Notice how, trying to impress this importance upon you, we strain to make strong metaphor: metaphors are the foundation stones of a building; they're the pumping hearts of literary writing. The ability to make metaphor is the most basic constituent of human thought and language. Yet, too often we leave direct consideration of these devices to the poets.

While essays can be organized many ways—through topic, chronology, or passage of time—organization through image and metaphor has become much more common. Clustering thoughts through images and loose associations (and metaphors are, at the most basic level, associations) seems fundamental to the way the human mind works. You may mentally jump from a look at a leaky faucet to a memory of watching the 1970s TV show "Charlie's Angels" because of the name of the actress Farrah Fawcett. You may then glide effortlessly from that thought to a sense memory of the powdered hot chocolate with marshmallows your mother made for you on weeknights while you watched television. As we grow more aware of and sophisticated about the way human consciousness operates, it makes sense that our literature will come closer to these basic thought rhythms. In the Beard excerpt we used earlier in this chapter, within a few sentences we see images of daggers and hissing and the use of the word *fire*. The imagery in this essay tells its own story—of a deadly event about to overtake the lives of these people.

You can often find clues to your own imagistic or metaphoric organizations when you recall the sensory association a thought or experience calls to mind. If the summer your best friend was killed in a diving accident always comes back to you with a whiff of honeysuckle, stay with that image and explore it in writing for a while. Does it lead to concepts of sweetness, youth, temptation, the quick blooming? If you let yourself write about the image alone for a while—not rushing to get to the subject your mind may insist is "the real story"—a more complex, more true, series of themes in your story will probably emerge.

The Rhythm of Your Sentences

It's a well-known fact that sentences must contain some variation. You must have become acquainted with this fact already. It's clear if you read a certain kind of prose. A work must use different kinds of sentence structures. Different kinds of sentence structures help alleviate that numbing feeling. It's a feeling you don't want your readers to have.

The previous paragraph contains six sentences, each composed of about ten words, and each is a simple sentence, beginning with a subject and its verb. Unlike this sentence you're currently reading, none begins with a clause. None is short. None, unlike the twenty-five-word sentence introducing this second paragraph, engages us for very long. Read both of these paragraphs together. Do you sense a difference? Do you, as we do, begin to go blank by the middle of the first paragraph, and finally feel some relief at the second one?

Notice that the second paragraph in this section of the book, while clarifying many of the ideas that the first paragraph contains, varies sentence structure and length. It also varies voice. One sentence uses the *vocative* or *command* voice ("Read both paragraphs together"), two are cast in the *interrogative* voice—they ask questions. Clauses like "Unlike this sentence" and "as we do" appear at the beginnings, middles, and ends of sentences to break up that repetitive simple structure.

There's a reason children and parents howl at each other, "Stop *saying* that!" Nothing's more boring than a voice repeating "Clean your room!" over and over again. Or the acquaintance who says "like" again and again, or the child banging out "Chopsticks" on the piano for the hundredth time. Nothing drives us quite as numbly mad as repetition does. Sentence structure is the poetic line, the bass and rhythm, of your prose. Riff, experiment, break it up.

TRY IT

1. Go through a piece of your writing and find a passage of summary that could or maybe even should be in scene. Don't fret right now about whether scene is absolutely necessary here: the point is to develop the skill of automatically asking yourself whether that option will help you.

Sometimes we stymie ourselves by imagining we must remember *everything* or we can't describe *anything*. So work with what you do remember. You may forget the look of a room but remember the sound or smell of it (think of Selzer's defining silence in that hospital room). Or create a bridge, such as writing a few sentences about how this is what a dialogue sounds like in your memory as you try to re-create it, giving yourself permission to fill in what you don't remember word for word. Remember that almost any device for reconstruction is fine, as long as you let readers in on what you're doing.

2. To get a feel for writing scene, re-create an event that took place in the last week—one with characters you can delineate and dialogue you can remember. It doesn't have to be important—it probably will help if it isn't. The point is simply to write two to three pages in which a location is established through description, people are characterized and talk, and something happens.

3. Finally, when you feel confident of your basic skills, remember a scene out of your own life that does contain the utmost importance. For everybody this will be different. It could be something as obviously important as the birth of a child or an argument leading to the end of a marriage; or its importance could be subtle but real to you—a conversation leading to a new closeness or a new distance between you and someone critical in your life. The point is, you must have a strong sense memory of this scene, one you can play back in your head over and over again; and it must matter to you.

Write the scene with as much fidelity as possible. Have the people in it enter and leave, describe what you saw, heard, and felt. If you still remember exactly how your mother asked, "Where were you last night?" describe the question in all the sensory detail you can muster, along with the wrench in your gut that came with it. Don't question right now why what matters matters. Trust your intuition, and tap into all of the passion you have invested in this scene.

Now question yourself. Why was a certain gesture or inflection so important? Why did you spend most of this conversation staring at a loudly ticking clock on the wall? Why did you notice the caramel color of your drink? The chances are that, like Selzer and Beard, your emotional story is locked into the details you remember of your life. When you begin to question the scene in this way, scrutinizing every detail, you'll probably discover an essay waiting to be written about this crucial moment.

4. Write a portrait or character sketch. Think of someone close to you and try to convey their essence, through clothing, sound, dialogue, gestures, and so forth, in two or three paragraphs. Don't aim to write scene; this portrait doesn't need to contain action, merely characterization.

When you're reasonably finished, trade your piece with a writing partner. Read each other's sketches and then elaborate on the person described, giving an overall, abstract sense of that individual's personality. How close did you come? Discuss with your partner ways this sketch could be refined: important details that may have been omitted, or others that could be misleading. Is this character sketch on its way to becoming an essay? Articulate to yourself why this character matters, why she is different, or why he is intriguingly typical.

5. Write a page or two of dialogue. Practice for this by using your notebook to record snippets of speech verbatim: exchanges with classmates, friends, spouses, parents. Pay attention to the syntax of speech. How much is grammatically correct or incorrect? How much slang or dialect appears in different speakers' voices? When you feel ready, write a page or two of typical dialogue—you can record it and write it down, or try to re-create it—with someone fairly close to you. Do the same partner swap with this dialogue you did with characterization, and see how much of the person you're describing comes through in his or her voice.

6. The only way to fully understand point of view is to experiment with it. Pull out an earlier essay of yours, or write a simple paragraph about some subject you've thought about as a likely one. Then recast the point of view, from first to second or third. Force yourself to keep going through at least one paragraph; don't look at the clunkiness of a sentence such as "For five years you lived in Alaska" and give up. Push through, and open yourself up to moments when the point of view works, when you feel interesting possibilities arise. (You can also refer to Chapter 10, "The Lyric Essay.")

Traditionally, point-of-view *shifting*—moving from the narrative position of one character to another within a piece—has been a problem area for fiction writers. Unintentional shifting is a common error for young writers; masterful shifts can make a story, as in Flannery O'Connor's famous shift to the Misfit's point of view at the end of "A Good Man Is Hard to Find." As nonfiction expands its reach, we see point of view shifting in this genre as well. Richard Selzer does it, as we've shown earlier in this chapter. See if such a switch can enrich a piece of your own writing.

7. Do a quick diagnostic of two to three paragraphs of your own prose (less might not be representative enough). How long do your sentences tend to be? How do you structure them? Do you vary voices or speech acts, such as questioning, stating, and commanding, or do you simply use the declarative or simple statement voice? Challenge yourself to approach a piece of prose in a way you haven't in the past—more short sentences or sentence fragments, perhaps, or more shifts in voice. See how this change alters your work, and opens up the possibilities of the essay.

13

The Writing Process and Revision

The writing has changed, in your hands, and in a twinkling, from an expression of your notions to an epistemological tool. The new place interests you because it is not clear. You attend. In your humility, you lay down the words carefully, watching all the angles. Now the earlier writing looks soft and careless. Process is nothing; erase your tracks. The path is not the work. I hope your tracks have grown over; I hope birds ate the crumbs; I hope you will toss it all and not look back.

—ANNIE DILLARD

In graduate school, I once submitted a workshop story that nobody liked—not one person. I remember one woman in particular: she dangled my work in front of her and said, her lips curling in distaste, "I don't understand why this story even exists!" Of course, at the time, I huffed and I puffed, and I spoke derisively of this woman at the bar that night. My friends cooed words of support, patted me on the back, and scanned the bar for more lively companionship. But even as I walked home that night, I could tell that her comment, though poorly worded, had something in it I needed to hear. It has stayed with me throughout the years, and now, when I'm at the final stage of revision, it's her question I hear in my head: Why does this essay exist? *I go back to work with a grim determination. No longer do I coddle the newborn prose, but hold it up roughly, probing for weakness, drawing blood. I try to identify and slash out all that is mere indulgence and platitude.*

At this stage in the writing process, the draft becomes nothing more than a fruitful scavenging ground. Right now, as I write, I'm in the middle of

Wyoming, and down the road a huge junkyard lies at the intersection of two minor highways. Against the rolling fields of wheat grass, this junkyard rises as ten acres of glinting metal, bent chrome, colors of every hue. One of my fellow colonists, a sculptor, began buying scraps to incorporate in her work: gorgeous landscapes with ribbons of rusted metal juxtaposed across blue skies. Now I've come to see the junkyard as a place of infinite possibility. What useful parts still hum in the innards of these machines? How will they be unearthed? What kind of work would it take to make them shine?

—BRENDA

The Drafting Process

Writing is easy; all you do is sit staring at a blank sheet of paper until the drops of blood form on your forehead.

—GENE FOWLER

When you first sit down to work, you may have no idea what the writing will bring. Maybe it even scares you a little, the thought of venturing into that unknown territory. Perhaps you circle your desk a while, wary of the task at hand. You pick up your cup of coffee in two hands and gaze out the window; you remember a letter you meant to write, an e-mail you meant to answer. You get up and check the mailbox, picking a few dead leaves off the coleus plant in the window. You sit down. You get up and change your shirt, appraise yourself in the mirror a long time, and come back to your desk. Maybe you pick up a book of poetry and read a few lines, put it down. You pick up your pen and write a word, then another. You go back and erase. You begin again.

Or maybe you are the type of writer who can sit down and start writing without hesitation, training yourself to write at least one full paragraph before stopping. You know you'll go back and trim and revise, so you just keep the words coming. You give yourself one hour, and you don't move from your chair in all that time. That hour, if the writing goes well, turns into two or three. You work steadily and pile up the pages.

Either way, the important thing to know, for yourself, is your own style. In the first case, to the untrained eye you may appear engaged in nothing but mere procrastination; certainly you are not writing. But if you know yourself well, you understand that this puttering is essential to your writing process. Some thought has been brewing in your brain now for several days, perhaps weeks, or months. This idea needs your body to occupy itself while the essay forms itself into something fleshy and sturdy enough to survive outside the mind and on the bleak terrain of the page. Or, in the second case, you act more like an athlete in training, knowing that routine and discipline are essential for your creative process. You write quickly because that's the only way for you to outrun your inner critic. Neither way is "correct." The only correct way to write is the way that works for you.

The writing process is just that: a *process*. You must have the patience to watch the piece evolve, and you need an awareness of your own stages. You must know when you can go pell-mell with the heat of creation, and when you must settle down, take a wider view, and make some choices that will determine the essay's final shape.

First drafts can be seen as "discovery drafts"; much of the writing you did from the prompts in Part 1 will fall into this category. You are writing to discover what you know or to recover memories and images that may have been lost to you. You are going for the details, the unexpected images, or the story line that reveals itself only as you go along. The best writing you do will have this sense of exploration about it; you allow yourself to go into the unknown, to excavate what lies beneath the surface. It's important to allow yourself permission to write *anything* in a first draft; otherwise you might censor yourself into silence. The first draft is the place where you just might light upon the right *voice* for telling this particular story; once you're onto that voice, you can write for hours.

No matter how good (or bad) this material seems at first glance, most often it will need some shaping and revision before it is ready for public eyes. Writer Natalie Goldberg calls revision "envisioning again," and this gets at the heart of true revision: you see your work in a new light and rework it for a specific effect. Revision, perhaps, is an acquired taste, but you may find that revision actually becomes the most "creative" part of creative nonfiction. At this stage you've already produced the raw material; now you have the opportunity to dig into it with your sleeves rolled up, all your tools sharpened and at the ready. It is in revision that the real work begins. The short story writer Raymond Carver often wrote twenty to thirty drafts before he was satisfied. "It's something I love to do," he said, "putting words in and taking words out." Or listen to Vladimir Nabokov: "I have re-written—often several times—every word I have ever published. My pencils outlast their erasers."

Global Revision Versus Line Editing

Revision can often be mistaken for line editing. There is a time, naturally, for going back to your prose to fine-tune the grammar, change a few words, and fix typos. But first you need to look at the essay as a whole and decide what will make this essay matter. What is the *real* subject of the piece? Where does the voice ring out most strongly? What image takes on more metaphorical significance than you realized? What now seems superfluous, mere deadweight that hinders the essay's momentum?

It's beneficial to take some time between drafts at this stage of the process. After that first, heady flush of creation settles down, you'll better be able to pinpoint the areas that sing and those that fall flat. You'll be able to notice an unexpected theme that emerges organically through the imagery you chose. You'll hear how the ending may actually be the beginning of your piece. Or the beginning may make for a better end. At this point you need to see the work as a fluid thing, with infinite possibilities still to come. What you may have intended to write may not be the most interesting part of the essay now. Be open to what has developed in the writing process itself, and don't be afraid to cut out those areas that no longer work.

Ask yourself this question: what is the essence of the topic *for this particular essay*? Many times it's easy to think that we have to put in everything we know or feel about a topic in one essay. For instance, if you're writing about a big issue, such as sexual abuse in childhood, you may be tempted to write a gigantic essay that incorporates every incident, every feeling you ever had, and the entire cast of characters involved. Or if you're writing about a life-changing travel experience, you might feel you need to put in every stop along the way. You have to figure out what is necessary for this essay *and this essay alone*. You will write other essays about the topic, don't worry. As writer Natalie Goldberg put it, "Your main obsessions have power; they are what you will come back to in your writing over and over again. And you'll create new stories around them."

You may keep only a small portion of the original work, perhaps even just one line. But by doing this kind of pruning, you enable new, more beautiful and sturdy growth to emerge. Take comfort in knowing the old work may find its way into new essays yet to come. Keep a file on your desk or in your computer called "fragments." If it's hard for you to let go of a section completely, put it in this file and know that you will call it back sometime in the future, in a new incarnation. Time and again, we have found new homes for those bits and pieces of prose that just didn't work in their original homes.

The Role of the Audience

When you're writing a first draft, it's often necessary to ignore any concept of audience just so you can get the material out. An attentive audience, hanging on your every word, can be inhibiting at that stage of the writing process. But when you're revising, some concept of audience will help you gain the necessary distance to do the hard work that needs to get done. This audience can be a single person. What would your writing teacher from high school—the one who drove you into writing in the first place—think of this essay? Where would she say you're being lazy or timid? What would your most trusted friend say about that last paragraph? Sometimes by merely placing yourself in another person's perspective, the problems of the piece become readily apparent and you can fix them with ease.

Or the audience can be much larger. Many times, having some kind of reading venue or publication in mind can focus your attention in a way that nothing else can. Many towns have open-mike readings in cafés or bookstores where beginning and experienced writers are invited to read their work to an audience. If you are brave enough to commit yourself to reading one night, you will find yourself in a fever of revision, reading the piece aloud many times and getting every word just right. Or, you might decide that you're ready to start sending your work out for publication. Find one journal and read as many copies as you can, then revise your piece with this publication in mind. You'll surprise yourself with the focus you can generate once the piece leaves the personal arena and goes public.

Three Quick Fixes for Stronger Prose

After you've done the hard labor on your essay, you'll want to do the finish work, the small things that make the prose really shine. (We don't mean to suggest these two processes are mutually exclusive; naturally you will find yourself adjusting the prose as you go along.) We have three quick fixes that make any piece stronger: "search and destroy," "the adjective/adverb purge," and "the punch."

Search and Destroy

The most overused verbs in the English language are variations of *to be*—these include *is*, *are*, *were*, *was*, and so forth. While these verbs are necessary (note how we just used two of them in the last two sentences), often you can sharpen your prose by going over the piece carefully and eliminating as many of them as you can. To do this you will need to look closely at the words surrounding the *to be* verbs; often you can find a stronger verb to take its place or a more juicy noun. Even when you eliminate an *is* here or a *was* there, the resultant prose will seem much cleaner and lighter. It's the kind of work the reader won't notice directly (except for word nuts like us), but it will immediately professionalize your prose.

Take a draft of an essay that is nearly finished. Go through it and, with a red pen, circle all the *to be* verbs. Go back and see if you can rework any of those sentences to replace them with verbs that feel more "muscled," have more impact to them. Sometimes you'll find you don't need the sentence at all, and you'll have eliminated some deadweight. If you're working in a group, exchange essays with one another and do the same thing. Suggest new lines that eliminate the *to be* verbs.

The Adjective/Adverb Purge

Often, adjectives can be your enemy rather than your friend. Adjectives or adverbs can act as crutches, holding up weak nouns or verbs, and they actually water down your prose rather than intensify it. As with the search-and-destroy exercise above, the point here is not to eliminate adjectives and adverbs altogether, but to scrutinize every one and see if it's necessary for the point you want to get across.

Take an essay you think is nearly finished and circle every adjective and adverb. Go back and see if you can rework the sentences to eliminate these words and replace them with stronger verbs and/or nouns. Or you can take stronger measures. For at least one writing session, ban adjectives and adverbs from your vocabulary. See how this exercise forces you to find more vivid nouns and verbs for your prose.

The Punch

Professional writers develop a fine ear for language. Writers are really musicians, aural artists attuned to every rhythm and nuance of their prose. And when you study the writers you admire, you'll invariably find that they tend to end most of their sentences, all of their paragraphs, and certainly the closing line of the essay, with potent words that pack a punch. They do not allow their sentences to trail off but close them firmly and strongly, with words that leave the reader satisfied. When you work toward strong closing words in your sentences, the prose also takes on a new sense of momentum and trajectory, the sentences rearranging themselves in fresh ways to wield that satisfying "crack."

Read your essay aloud, paying attention to the sounds of the words at the ends of sentences and paragraphs. Do they ring clearly and cleanly, firmly ending your thought? Or do they trail off in abstraction? Circle any words that seem weak to you; then go back and rework these sentences for better closing effects. Pay particular attention to the word you use to end the entire essay. How do you leave your reader? What will he remember?

An Example of the Writing Process

We asked the writer Bernard Cooper for his thoughts on the writing process. Here is what he had to say:

A friend of mine once said that she needed two things in order to write: paper, and Liquid Paper. This was before she used a computer, of course, but I think her statement illustrates the importance of revision, the necessity to change and perfect what one has written down. I edit relentlessly— have already revised this very statement. My prose itself tends to come in short bursts, while the bulk of my time is involved in trying different words and sentence structures and punctuation so those word-bursts say exactly what I want them to. Revision seems to me the writer's most crucial task; you are given the chance to make your work as powerful as possible. "Words are all we have," said novelist Evan Connell, "and they'd better be the right ones." Anyone who has written for long knows the pleasure in finding the word that makes a description suddenly more vivid, or finding the structure that makes a sentence more taut, surprising, rhythmic, or funny.

When you write well, revision becomes not a chore, but the essence of the writing act itself. What came before cleared the way for what is to come; no writing is ever wasted, no time spent at the desk useless. Writing creates its own rhythm and momentum, and you must be willing to go with it, to become absorbed in the task, to let go of the writing you once thought precious. It's exhausting work, requiring stamina and rigor, but the rewards keep you going.

At one time or another, many writers experience what they call "gifts"— essays or poems or stories that seem to come effortlessly, full-blown onto the page with little revision or effort. But as the poet Richard Hugo put it, "Lucky accidents seldom happen to writers who don't work. . . . The hard work you do on one poem is put in on all poems. The hard work on the first poem is responsible for the sudden ease of the second. If you just sit around waiting for the easy ones, nothing will come. Get to work."

TRY IT

1. Take a writing session to observe everything you do around writing. What is your routine? How does it serve or sabotage you? What keeps you from writing? What helps you? What happens when you change your routine?

2. Do you have an inner critic that immediately censors or criticizes your writing? Take a piece of paper and draw a line down the center. On the right side of the paper, begin writing, perhaps from one of the writing exercises in Part 1. On the left side, write down any critical thoughts that come to mind as you write. (Don't worry if the session becomes only critical thoughts; it happens all the time!) Do this for about five or ten minutes, then go back and read what the critic has to say to you.

On a new sheet of paper, begin a dialogue with your inner critic. How does the critic both enable and sabotage your writing? For example, you may realize that the critic is merely trying to protect you from the harsh criticism the world might heap on you; rather than a hostile presence, the critic may actually be quite benevolent.

3. Take out a piece you wrote at least a month ago. Read it aloud, either to yourself or to a kind audience. Make note of the paragraphs that feel full and rich and those that are not as strong. Are there any areas that surprise you? What is the essay *really* about? What can be cut out and saved for another time? What needs to be included that was left out at first?

Here are some specific questions to ask yourself as you go about the global revision process:

- Is there one image that can be used as a cohesive thread throughout the piece? How can you amplify this image and transform it from beginning to end?
- Have you chosen the most effective point of view for telling the story? What happens when you experiment with third person? Second person?
- Look closely at the beginning paragraph of your essay. Do you begin in a way that draws the reader in? Often, the first few paragraphs of a rough draft act as "clearing the throat." Is the true beginning really a few pages in?
- Look closely at the end of the essay. Do you end in a way that leaves the reader with a compelling image? Often it's tempting to "sum up" the essay in a way that can be wholly unsatisfying to the reader. Can you end on an image rather than an idea?
- How do the beginning and ending paragraphs mirror or echo one another? The first and last paragraphs act as a frame for the piece as a whole. They

are, in a way, the most important places in the essay, because they determine everything that happens in between. If you make an effort to connect them in some way—repeating a key image from the beginning, bringing back on stage the major players for a final bow—you will find a stunning finish to the piece.

14

The Writing Group

The fiction that artistic labor happens in isolation, and that artistic accomplishment is exclusively the provenance of individual talents, is politically charged and, in my case at least, repudiated by the facts. While the primary labor on *Angels* has been mine, more than two dozen people have contributed words, ideas and structures to these plays.

—TONY KUSHNER

I have just received a joyous e-mail from my friend Dan, telling me he has placed his latest manuscript with a university press he admires. It is an outpouring of both personal and group pride. My husband and I have been part of Dan's writing life for more than a decade, since the two of us met him in graduate school. That was fourteen years ago.

Originally, a group of six graduate students comprised our workshop. I can't remember whose casual suggestion it was that we begin meeting in a special room in a Charlottesville tavern that's always been something of a grad student hangout. The small room holds old Moët & Chandon Champagne posters crammed on every wall, curvy Art Deco women holding bottles. Each piece we put up for discussion we distribute the week before and talk about for twenty minutes to half an hour. The feedback is smart, bracing, encouraging. We find both value in everything and room for the writing to flower into something even finer. And, of course, there's always time for chat and catching up before and after the workshop part of our get-togethers. In addition to our workshop meetings, we soon celebrate each other's successes, throw each other parties, help each other search out publication venues.

Now, almost a decade and a half later, we have mail and e-mail. We still share our work, albeit less regularly and much more slowly. We still feel a kudo for one of us is a kudo for the group, as we have nurtured, edited, and prodded each other for much of our writing careers. Between us we've gone from beginners at the art of literary writing to having published twelve books. And all of us know, as Dan's e-mail shows, we couldn't have done it alone.

—SUZANNE

The Need for Feedback

Tony Kushner, in the quote introducing this chapter, states the case strongly but not, we think, too strongly. Writers need feedback. The myth of writers as loners who follow their vision and remain true to their inner muse, bucking rather than embracing outside help, is very much a myth. It was created largely by the writers of the British Romantic period, whose artistic mythologies we still cling to, though those writers themselves used one another unceasingly as idea sources and sounding boards. Virtually all writers do. "I write," said Terry Tempest Williams, "in a solitude born out of community."

The modern writing workshop or writing group is not an innovation but a form of learning that can be traced back as long as literature and the arts have flourished. You can use this chapter to find ways to create your own workshop group—one with members you trust, who can grow with you and your work—or to get the most productive working relationship you can out of the group you have. Even if this desire seems improbable now, trust us: if you keep writing, you will want caring and responsive readers.

Setting Guidelines for Discussion:
A Practice Approach

In the following section on learning to give useful responses, we will provide very specific suggestions for shaping workshop discussion. You may use or adapt these as your group sees fit. For now, it is a good idea to have a preliminary talk with your peers about what does or does not work for you as a group in receiving feedback. You can and should discuss the entire process of workshopping, come up with a procedure, and devise your own workshop etiquette—a collective sense of what is OK and not OK in talking about your writing. Logistical questions to discuss include how far in advance you will share your work, whether you will read pieces aloud at any point, and whether you want to include written comments or limit yourself to oral critique.

It is essential to find a method of discussion with which the group feels safe and comfortable; don't flounder around trying to shape your valuable writing without first defining what helps you. To guide this process, find an essay, perhaps from a literary magazine, for practice. Read the piece and offer comments as you would in a workshop setting, and together monitor the discussion for responses that seem diminishing, unconstructive, or unhelpful. You may want to ask the group to rule out feedback based on "I do like," "I don't like" formulas. These are by their very nature subjective comments and hard to use in the revision process. All of you together can watch out for unhelpful critical language—"stinks," "lame," "one cliché after another."

Of course we don't advocate only praise; those words probably do hold suggestions for revisions that need to be made. What's important is that you work together as a group to find more constructive approaches. "This doesn't come up to the level of the rest of the essay," "I'm not seeing this scene yet," or "The language here could be more original" might be suitable comments to replace the offending ones.

Even when you hear responses that feel appropriate, use this practice session to sharpen them. If someone says he or she can't quite get a feel for a character, question why that is and try to formulate the most specific response possible. "I can't quite see David because he's never described and never speaks until you find him crying in the kitchen." Try reformulating your feedback comments two and three times to make them as specific as possible. Practice together until you feel good about one another's feedback style and the comments flowing from your discussion feel supportive, encouraging, and full of ideas to take back to your writing desk.

The Agenting Approach

One workshop strategy we have had great success with is the agenting approach. It is a role-play method. All the members of the writing group agree to function as one another's literary agents for the duration of the group.

Literary agents take on their author-clients because they believe in them. Agents feel certain they can sell their clients' essays and books. They derive their income from sales of their authors' work, so their faith in their authors is concrete and tangible. At the same time, agents become valuable critics and editors. They must bring their clients' work to the publishing market in its finest possible form.

As literary agents, then, you believe absolutely in one another and in the value of the group members' writing, and the fact that it can be brought to a final, polished form worthy of publication. At the same time you have an interest in making the essay or book extract the best it can be. And so you will provide substantial encouragement and substantial feedback.

As an agent your comments are always couched in terms like, "I think this will really work once the dialogue feels more authentic/Jack has a fuller character/we know where Luke ended up." Like an agent, you will always begin your responses by citing what *does* work, and, where appropriate, providing ideas for transferring that success to less polished parts of the essay.

When beginning this approach, it can help to write out comments in the form of letters—the type of communication you'd likely get from a literary agent. These letters will begin with an affirmation of your faith in your client; a summary of what works well in the piece; and a careful, detailed listing of what needs to be addressed before the piece is finally ready. These letters can be used to fuel discussion and passed to the author at the end of a workshop session. A wonderful side benefit of the agenting approach can be, when you reach a phase in your group relationship where lots of revision has taken place, you can decide to devote an hour or two to browsing at the periodical section of a bookstore or a library, finding suitable publication venues for one another's work.

Avoid broad comments and responses that simply provide your evaluation, your stamp of approval: "I liked this," "I couldn't get into this." Use language that reflects your awareness that your opinion is simply your opinion, not the word of a literary judge speaking from on high. Try to use language that addresses the problem: "This feels sketchy to me," not "This is weak writing." Be as specific as you possibly can. Always include in your discussions a session, either at the beginning or the end, where you only talk about what works well in the piece. It's too easy for workshop conversations to become centered wholly on the negative.

Here are a few more guidelines to consider.

- Don't use pointlessly critical language.
- Don't be subjective or start talking about your own experience unless there's a specific reason to, such as an expert knowledge you can add to the work at hand. ("I've worked at an emergency room and I don't think it would be painted bright pink," not "I've worked at an emergency room; isn't it weird?")
- When you give praise, see if you can add even more to your comment by suggesting another place where the same writing tactics can help the essay. Do provide revision suggestions freely, along with support and encouragement. The other side of the workshop coin from the pick-it-all-apart session is the lovefest, which ultimately disrespects the writer's ability to bring his work to a higher level, and does him no good.

Remember always that as you give to others in your group, you will get back. You have a deep commitment to their growth as writers and to the productive workings of the group as a whole, so always act accordingly. Also, we often learn the most about our own writing while listening carefully to critiques about someone else's work. What is true for that person struggling with a satisfying ending is probably true for you as well. Don't assume that the only time you learn anything is when your own piece is up for discussion.

Here are a few tips for making the group work.

- **Agree to distribute copies of writing to be workshopped no less than forty-eight hours in advance of your meeting.** Provide photocopies or laser-printed copies, not handwritten ones that will be hard to read professionally. Even with all the goodwill in the world, things come up, and with less than two days to prepare comments, members will come in scanning the essays as they go, a frustrating experience for reader and author.

• **Set an amount of time you will spend on each essay, with a five- or ten-minute degree of flexibility.** Twenty minutes to half an hour usually works.

• **Have one of you agree to facilitate the discussion.** Facilitating means making sure the conversation stays within or lasts until the assigned period. Facilitators can also throw out topics or questions as necessary (each piece under discussion can have a different facilitator). We remember one poorly run graduate workshop in which the instructor simply allowed the group to go on as little or as long as it liked, leading to discussions that ranged anywhere from five minutes to an hour. That's a frustrating, insulting experience for an author, so agree in advance to monitor your time and keep comments on track.

A Workshop Checklist

Here is an intuitive way to read an essay to be discussed:

1. Jot down the scenes, descriptions, and images that stick with you: the "Velcro words and phrases," as writer and teacher Sheila Bender put it. Put the essay down and make note of the first thing you remember about it. Generally these passages are the ones that not only are the best written, but the most key to what the essay is doing at a deep level.

2. Identify the emotional tones of the essay and its prose. You may sense the pleasure of a friend's visit, of a hike, the anxiety of sentences that all begin with "I think" or "I believe." Do you get the sense of over formality in a phrase like "I am perturbed"? Do you wonder why the author calls her mother by the definite article, "the mother"? Does it feel somewhat chilly? In all cases, are these feelings ones the author intended to convey, or do they seem unintentional and perhaps working against the movement of the essay?

3. Identify your curiosity. Make note of where specifically you want to know more. "I want to know more about that distant definite-article mother," "about that feeling of perturbation in the pit of the stomach," "about the author's uncertainty," "about the rest of the family," and so forth. Which locations/characters would benefit from more description? Which characters' voices do you want to hear? Where do you want to know more about the

author's responses and feelings? These curiosities help locate places for expansion.

If you need help going deeper with your comments, here are some **content questions** to consider:

- What is the organizing force of the essay, and does it sustain the piece? If this essay has a clear narrative (a story to tell), is the story clear? If it is a lyric essay organized around images, do the images keep it going?
- Are characters effectively presented and fully developed?
- Is dialogue believable, important to the overall essay, and used where it needs to be? Does it help shape character?
- Are there places where exposition should be replaced by scene for greater reader involvement or scene replaced by exposition for greater compression?
- Is the point of view working well? Would it help to try another point of view, e.g., substitute first person for second?
- If this is a meditation or essay of ideas, is there an ideology behind it? Is it presented clearly? Is it presented in a way that respects the reader, rather than becoming preachy or heavy-handed?
- Are the images used fresh and interesting? Do they work together in a way that supports the essay?
- Is the language fresh throughout, avoiding sentimentality and cliché?

Here are some **form questions** to keep in mind:

- Does the form of the essay add to/enhance its content?
- Is the organization effective? Look closely at elements such as collaging, the use of white space "jumps" between material, and whether the piece's organization is purely chronological, following the order in which events happened, or something else.
- Does the piece begin and end in a way that feels satisfying? Note that "satisfying" does not necessarily mean providing closure, or full answers to any questions it might raise. Does the essay open in a way

that makes you want to keep reading, and end in a way that provides some sort of aesthetic stopping point?

These samples will help you with **diction questions**:

- Does the language seem appropriate to the subject? Is it at times overly fussy or formal or overly slangy and flip?
- Does the essay contain any archaic or outmoded language—a trap we all fall into in literary writing—that doesn't belong?
- Are the sentence structures and rhythms appealing and effective?

We suggest you use these questions when you read, picking and choosing as seems appropriate, rather than marching through them one by one in the group. Facilitators can also keep this checklist handy, as a way of sparking conversation when it begins to lag.

Creating Your Own Writing Group

The veteran publisher Stanley Colbert wrote, "Your journey to the best-seller list begins with a single reader." All of the people you come in contact with who share your interest in writing and literature are resources for forming a writing group.

Who are your friends or acquaintances who love to write? If you've never talked with them about forming a response group, try it. Most writers spend their lonely computer or typewriter time dreaming of an audience of enthusiastic readers—chances are, you will be proposing something they'll regard as a dream come true. If you're shy about your writing and find it hard to think about sharing it with your cat, let alone a group, try this. Look at the questions in the intuitive list, given previously in this chapter. Now think of a piece of your writing and imagine answers to those questions. Chances are the thought of hearing a list of your Velcro scenes and images, the places you've made a reader curious, will actually seem pretty pleasant.

The fact is, when we worry about sharing our work, we imagine ourselves handing an essay to someone and saying, "What do you think?" and standing, knees trembling, for the final judgment. Well, first of all, no one has the all-knowing literary judgment to do that (a contemporary of poet John Milton, author of *Paradise Lost*, wrote of him, "His fame is gone out like a candle in a snuff and his memory will always stink"). Second of all, delivery of verdicts is not what writing groups are for, and you should never let yours drift into that destructive habit. Remember, you can and should exert control about the feed-back process, and talk about it as a group until you get it right.

Kate Trueblood, an author and teacher of writing, formed a group with three other writers she knew who seemed compatible. Though the group was friendly and supportive, the workshop did spend a few meetings having to fine-tune their discussion style. "At first it was a little jumbled and unfocused, and feelings were hurt," Kate remembers. The group communally generated a list of rules that's kept them going successfully for many years now. "We talk about what's successful first, then acknowledge amongst ourselves when we're moving to critique. We work from global issues to smaller issues. And each time we pass out a manuscript we designate what kind of feedback we want, and what stage the work is in."

If you don't know anyone interested enough or compatible enough to form a workshop group with you, you still have another excellent resource—your local bookstore. It's a well-kept secret that many bookstores have active writing groups that meet regularly and often welcome new members. Our town has a writing group that meets once or twice a month at a local Barnes & Noble. New members join by making a phone call to the group's founder and coordinator, who makes sure they are serious and committed to the group's style before letting them in.

If you find your bookstore(s) does not have a workshop group, start one. Ask to speak to the store manager of a bookstore you like or, in a larger store, the community relations coordinator. These folks will generally help you, by posting signs and advertising in store newsletters and calendars, to find other folks in your community interested in sharing their writing. From the inter-views we've done with bookstore personnel, the response will almost certainly be strong: there are a lot of writers seeking readers out there. From the book-store's point of view, it's a way to lure literature lovers into their store on a regular basis. From your point of view, it's heaven: a group of peer reviewers, and a comfy place to meet.

Most of all, be excited about one another's work, and your own. Use your writing group as a place to generate writing as well as to critique it. Set aside time to create writing prompts together, or agree to try separately to tackle a difficult subject, providing each other support as you go along. Have writing time together with music that inspires you playing in the background. Meet at museums. Bring a piece of writing each week you've fallen in love with and share it, then talk about what it can teach you.

Remember that a group of writing friends once sat in the house during a thunderstorm and challenged each other to write a ghost or horror story, and then met again to share their efforts, one of which was Mary Shelley's classic *Frankenstein*. It was a book that would never have been created any other way.

Last Words

Lately I've been reading the selected poems of William Stafford, which includes some of the poetry he wrote the year before he died. Stafford was in the habit of getting up every day at 4 A.M. He wrote, by hand, during the dark, quiet hours in his study. He wrote about the simple things, the small things, in a voice that carries with it that sense of early morning meditation.

I don't know if Stafford was cognizant of his approaching death (he was eighty years old, after all, and perhaps at some point we can no longer deny that particular specter at our door), but the poems written during those final days have the quality of "last words": stripped of artifice, speaking from a self that wants only to understand and be understood. These are poems that want us to pay attention—not to abstract ideas and philosophies, not to idle worries or regrets, but to the world as it unfolds before us, every minute, every day. And as I read these poems I'm thinking that all of our writing, perhaps, could be written with this kind of disposition: with the tenor of "last words," the essays we would leave behind if no further writing were possible.

—BRENDA

These days, whenever I visit one of my friends, her twelve-year-old daughter begs for my stories. My own son, at four-and-a-half, is already too jaded to listen to me for very long. But suddenly, my Baby Boom, New York–area history fascinates Elisabeth. I find it hard to come up with enough anecdotes to satisfy her curiosity. She's fascinated that I saw the Rolling Stones and the Grateful Dead when they were young bands; she fires questions at me about Apollo 11, or how I watched Richard Nixon's motorcade once as his thick makeup sweated down in the heat. She wants to know about the antiwar protests and race riots I grew up with. These are topics she's studying in school, and I reach deep into that trusty and unquestioned valise—my life—to find material to satisfy her.

It's hard to believe. Our lives—secret, banal, and full of Kleenexes and bus schedules as they are—form stepping-stones to the future and vital links to the past. What we have lived through and done will define the world as it exists hundreds of years from now. We are the only witnesses to this our time, which is as wondrous and banal as any moment in history, and which carries its full complement of world-changing events: wars fought, great art made, rights hard won. Value your own life and the experiences you've had: they are priceless. At the same time, learn to love the world you live in. Hike urban streets, mountain trails, or better yet, both. Go to places you've never thought of going before; talk to everyone you meet with the assumption that his life is just as interesting as yours. Fall in love, be passionate, and the stories of your time will be yours to tell.

—SUZANNE

Regaining Passion

Sometimes when you're in a writing class or studying writing intensively, it's easy to temporarily lose the passion that brought you to writing in the first place. It's easy to feel as though you've taken all the magic out of it, and you sit at your desk, bored or resistant, unable to find one thing worth writing about. Especially when you write creative nonfiction, it's easy to feel as though you've "used up" all your material, plumbed all your memories, reflected on everything there is to reflect about. Your mirror has lost its luster, your pen run dry of ink.

When this happens (and it happens to all of us), you must do whatever it takes to refill the well. This might mean just taking some time out to roam the city or spending a week on the couch with your favorite books and comfort food. It might mean making a date with your writing group or deciding to write poetry or fiction for a while instead. The important thing to remember is *it will come back*. Your passion for writing will always return, doubled in force, after its period of dormancy. The writing life is one of patience and faith.

As you've read through this book, you've received all kinds of writing prompts to trigger new work; you've read about techniques; you've learned a bit about the philosophical and ethical challenges of creative nonfiction. You've perhaps learned new ways to approach your own memories, research interests, and ideas. Now, with all this knowledge still settling inside your head, we will tell you one last thing:

Forget it all.

Don't forget it forever. But just forget it for now. Take a moment to be quiet in the space where you do your best work, at the time when the muses are most present. Try to remember what it's like to be a beginner; regain what the Zen masters call "beginner's mind," open to all possibility. When you're ready, we offer you this one last

TRY IT

1. What are your "last words"? What would you write if you knew your time was up?

2. What would you notice in the world around you? What's important for us to hear?

Bibliography

What Should I Read Now, and Where Can I Find It?

Read, read, read. Read everything—trash, classics, good, and bad,
and see how they do it. Just like a carpenter who works as an
apprentice and studies the master. Read! You'll absorb it. Then write.
If it is good, you'll find out. If it's not, throw it out the window.
                                        —WILLIAM FAULKNER

There's no getting around it. Reading and writing go hand in hand. You cannot be a good writer without also being a good reader. You *must* read widely,
with the eye of a writer, engrossed not only in the plot or the characters or
the descriptions, but attuned to the craft that makes these things come alive
on the page. You read to hear other writers' voices, but you also read to tune
up your *own* voice, to remember what gets you excited about writing in the
first place. Through reading, you continually learn the craft all over again.

Throughout *Tell It Slant*, we refer to many fine essays to illustrate key
points in writing creative nonfiction. Space and money prohibit the inclusion
of those essays in this book, but we've compiled a handy list for you to keep
in mind the next time you're prowling the bookstore. This is by no means a
comprehensive accounting of great creative nonfiction! Such a list would be
long and wide, but we hope to give you at least a place to begin.

Atwood, Margaret. "Nine Beginnings." In *The Writer on Her Work*, edited by Janet Sternberg. New York: W.W. Norton, 1991.

This essay is written in the form of an interview with one question: "Why do you write?" The title and form also suggest that the reader is privy to first drafts fished out of the wastebasket. In a way, we are pulled into the "interview" as well, forced to think about our own reasons for writing. Though Atwood initially resists answering the question, she does, in fact reveal quite a bit about herself and her writing, ending in a section that could be taken as a complete writing philosophy.

Baker, Will. "My Children Explain the Big Issues." In *In Short: A Collection of Brief Creative Nonfiction*, edited by Judith Kitchen and Mary Paumier Jones. New York: W.W. Norton, 1996.

In this short essay, Will Baker gives us several vignettes about his children. These sections all have subtitles using abstract concepts such as fate, feminism, and so forth. The author himself makes no commentary on the small scenes; instead the reader must put together meaning based on the title and the subtitles. Like Atwood's "Nine Beginnings," this essay is a good model for looking at how writers use unconventional means to deal with transitions from topic to topic, or from scene to scene.

Baldwin, James. "Notes of a Native Son." In *Notes of a Native Son*, revised edition. Boston: Beacon Press, 1984.

In this famous essay, originally published in 1955, Baldwin not only articulates part of his autobiography, but he also sets this autobiographical material against the backdrop of history (the race riots) and the issue of racism. As Henry Louis Gates, Jr., put it, Baldwin "named for me the things you feel but couldn't utter. . . . Jimmy's essays articulated for the first time to white America what it meant to be American and a black American at the same time."

Bausch, Richard. "So Long Ago." In *The Business of Memory*, edited by Charles Baxter. St. Paul: Graywolf Press, 1999.

Why do we remember the things we do? How are they distilled to stories in our minds and the stories we tell others? Is memory the "truth?" Bausch is primarily a fiction writer, so you might explore the fictional techniques at work in this essay: the use of scene, dialogue, narrative voice, and so forth. We are listening to a story: a story about the nature of story and memory. This personal, intimate stance seems as necessary to the essay as its content.

Beard, Jo Ann. "The Fourth State of Matter." In *The Boys of My Youth*. Boston: Little, Brown and Co., 1998.

This essay first appeared in the *New Yorker*'s special fiction issue for 1996, and many people assumed it to be a short story rather than an essay (some bookstores also wanted to display her subsequent collection of essays *The Boys of My Youth* in the fiction section rather than in nonfiction). What makes an essay read like an essay? What makes a story read like a story? What is the line between truth and fiction? Is there one? Do you read a piece differently if it's presented as fiction? These are the kinds of questions you can think about as you read this stunning piece.

Berry, Wendell. "An Entrance to the Woods." In *Recollected Essays 1965 1980*. San Francisco: North Point Press, 1981.

Wendell Berry is a farmer in Kentucky. He's also a poet (a famous one at that) but his primary orientation revolves around finding a home for himself in nature. His observations are not mere glorification but a profound call to awaken the reader to the encroachment of "civilization" on nature. You do not need to agree with Berry's politics to appreciate this particular style. Connections arise intuitively, through language.

Cooper, Bernard. "The Fine Art of Sighing." In *Truth Serum*. Boston: Houghton Mifflin Co., 1996. (Also reprinted in *In Short*.)

This short, perfect essay can illustrate many different aspects of effective creative nonfiction. It appears at the exact center of Cooper's collection *Truth Serum*, when he moves from essays that deal mainly with his childhood and into ones that deal with his adulthood as a gay male. The recurrent theme of the body runs throughout this collection. Cooper explores how he struggles to come to terms with his sexuality, with his fear of AIDS, and his relationships with men and women. The structure of "The Fine Art of Sighing" allows Cooper to approach big subjects in a *peripheral* way, sidling up to the issue of the body through the smallest gesture of the sigh.

Didion, Joan. "Goodbye to All That." In *Slouching Towards Bethlehem*. New York: Simon and Schuster, 1968.

Didion might be called a foremother of creative nonfiction. This essay is one of Didion's most well-known pieces; the title may be an allusion to Robert Graves's autobiography (published in 1929) in which he describes his experience as a young man in World War I. For both writers—Didion and Graves—the phrase "Goodbye to All That" sums up, in almost a breezy voice, the dismissal of youth from the perspective of the older (and wiser?) self. Didion is a novelist, journalist, and screenplay writer, as well as an essayist, and all these skills come to bear in her creative nonfiction writing. You can try imitating the long sentence in the first section that starts, "When I first saw New York." The long sentence tends to elicit strong details and memories that may otherwise remain hidden.

Dillard, Annie. "Total Eclipse." In *Teaching a Stone to Talk: Expeditions and Encounters*. New York: Harper & Row, 1982.

Annie Dillard gained fame as a creative nonfiction writer with her book *Pilgrim at Tinker Creek*, a book-length meditation on the spirituality and metaphysics inherent in nature. Dillard often turns toward the natural world in her attempts to make sense of the ideas that haunt her. In this essay, an eclipse becomes more than an eclipse; it becomes a terrifying metaphysical journey. From her personal perspective, Dillard also gives us many facts about eclipses embedded in the narrative.

Duncan, David James. "The Mickey Mantle Koan." In *River Teeth: Stories and Writings.* New York: Doubleday, 1995.

As we described earlier in the book, a "koan" is a Zen puzzle, a riddle given to a disciple by the master as a way of spurring enlightenment. Zen monks often work these koans for years, and the answers to them are most often illogical, defying logic or reason. In this essay, Duncan approaches a difficult subject—the death of his teenaged brother—by focusing on a small object that is peripheral to the main story: a baseball signed by Mickey Mantle. This object becomes his koan, something he doesn't quite understand. He uses the opportunity of the essay as a way of working out this koan on the page.

Fisher, M. F. K. "A Thing Shared." In *The Art of Eating.* New York: Collier Books, 1990.

In 1943, M. F. K. Fisher wrote, "There is a communion of more than our bodies when bread is broken and wine drunk. And that is my answer, when people ask me: Why do you write about hunger, and not wars or love?" Fisher is known primarily as a food writer, though her work takes on many more topics than food. She has written about highly personal subjects such as her divorce from her first husband and the death of her second. Her books often include recipes interspersed among the prose. Fisher shows how memories of particular tastes can be the key to highly charged memories.

Goldbarth, Albert. "After Yitzl." In *A Sympathy of Souls.* Minneapolis: Coffee House Press, 1990.

This braided essay explores how we create our own ancestries. Goldbarth is known primarily as a poet, and one who incorporates all manner of disciplines into his work: science, pop culture, film, and so forth. (He's also known as a collector of kitsch; he supposedly has the largest collection of 1950s outer-space toys in the state of Kansas!) His propensity for gathering disparate images is evident in this essay and may initially cause you some consternation. (His indulgent delight with language may also invite resistance!)

Hemley, Robin. "Reading History to My Mother." In *Fourth Genre: Explorations in Nonfiction*, edited by Michael Steinberg. East Lansing, MI: MSU Press, spring, 2001.

In this essay, Hemley approaches a difficult topic—taking care of an aging parent—through the form of a braided essay. He also uses a photograph as a way of entering a past not his own, and he publishes the photo along with the essay. Hemley once told us this essay seemed to come together almost magically, every piece falling into place. He wrote it while he was trying to figure out some complex issues surrounding his mother, and so it carries that kind of urgency, that quality of attention to intuition.

Iyer, Pico. "Where Worlds Collide." In *The Fourth Genre: Contemporary Writers of/on Creative Nonfiction*, edited by Robert Root and Michael Steinberg. Boston: Allyn and Bacon, 1999.

Pico Iyer is a huge fan of Van Morrison. We mention this because much of his work, though ostensibly about travel in the physical world, is also about interior, spiritual travels, journeys "into the mystic," as Morrison would put it. (Iyer has also spent quite a bit of time in monasteries.) This particular essay takes a commonplace locale, the airport, and transforms it through his attention to detail. He makes the familiar exotic; he makes us really *look* at sights we might readily pass over in our quest to get somewhere else.

Kingston, Maxine Hong. "No Name Woman." In *The Woman Warrior*. New York: Knopf, 1976.

This story within a story sets up a series of tensions, as various characters interact with the story of the aunt. "No Name Woman" serves as a brilliant introduction to the way family stories become mythological. They become springboards to the family members' feelings about themselves and one another. It also works as a meditation on the reliability of memory itself.

Kitchen, Judith. "Things of This Life." From *Only the Dance*. Columbia, S.C.: University of South Carolina Press, 1994.

This elegiac essay presents a writer connecting the curbed desires of adulthood with the seemingly limitless desires of childhood, and as such, it is an essay that unfolds through intimate detail. One of the most arresting choices Kitchen makes is to narrate this essay in the third person, a technique that we often forget is available to us even when writing about ourselves.

Lamott, Anne. "Why I Don't Meditate." In *The Best Spiritual Writing 1998*, edited by Philip Zaleski. San Francisco: HarperSanFrancisco, 1998.

This essay teeters on a fine balance between slapstick humor and its serious message of opening up and trying to connect, rather than letting life's difficulties and your own anxieties shut you down. It is about Lamott's lack of ability to meditate, much as she wants to, and her gradual opening up to a substitute path that serves her just as well.

Mukherjee, Bharati. "A Four-Hundred-Year-Old Woman." In *The Writer on Her Work*, edited by Janet Sternberg. New York: W.W. Norton, 1991.

Mukherjee invokes the haunting image of her father's native village in what was then India, now a place annexed to another country, for a descriptive yet philosophical meditation on the nature of home, or "desh." Mukherjee uses her upbringing—born in a place that no longer exists, taught in a Western school that inculcated in its students a culture foreign to their own—as a metaphor for the transplanted lives of many contemporary people.

Price, Jennifer. "A Brief Natural History of the Plastic Pink Flamingo." In *Flight Maps*. New York: Basic Books, 1999.

This essay is a well-researched and charming look at a quirky subject, plastic lawn flamingos. Though these flamingos might seem hardly worth such consideration, the author ties their swelling popularity in the mid-twentieth century with Americans' evolving attitudes toward nature—the desire to experience it in tamed, altered form. She pulls in periodicals and advertisements of the period, explaining how the lawn birds first became so popular—representing a serious commitment to a particular kind of "artificial nature"—then made the transition to the sort of jokey relic we call "kitsch."

Rekdal, Paisley. "The Night My Mother Met Bruce Lee." In *The Night My Mother Met Bruce Lee*. New York: Pantheon Books, 2000.

Rekdal, who is Chinese-Norwegian, spends much of her book exploring her relationship with her mother, whose ancestry is Chinese. She probes the deeper questions associated with being biracial, here seen in the delicate way she observes Chinese culture both from the inside and the outside. It's a beautiful example of how to deepen an essay by fully imagining the life of a person close to you, a person you seek to understand.

Sanders, Scott Russell. "Buckeye." In *Writing from the Center*. Bloomington, IN: Indiana University Press, 1995.

This short essay contains so much. It is both a character sketch and an extended memory, as the author uses the buckeyes he's saved from his father's pocket to conjure his father up in specific childhood scenes. The father is characterized physically—particularly through his laborer's hands—and in his voice. The essay relies on scene, detail, and dialogue to establish its beautiful, elegiac tone.

Sedaris, David. "The Drama Bug." In *Naked*. Rockland, MA: Wheeler Pub., 1997.

Nobody handles relationships quite like Sedaris, who manages to present his family in all of their rough-edged gruffness, yet keep his tone ultimately affirmative—of the possibilities of intimacy, of family. Sedaris also has a wonderful hand with dialogue; his remembered Shakespearean soliloquies are hilariously exaggerated. All of his books are available on audio; his reading style adds considerably to the humor of the essays.

Selzer, Richard. "The Knife." In *Mortal Lessons: Notes on the Art of Surgery*.
New York: Simon and Schuster, 1976.

Not only a vivid description of the feeling of surgery from a practicing surgeon and a fine scientific piece, but "The Knife" is also an extended experiment in point of view. Beginning impersonally—"One holds the knife"—the
essay shifts quickly to a first person—"I am still struck with a kind of
dread"—and then second, as the author moves deeper into this dangerous
surgery: "You turn aside to wash your gloves." Selzer removes the normal barrier between the reader and the experience, putting us in the position of fighting to save this desperately ill patient.

Sutin, Lawrence. *A Postcard Memoir*. St. Paul: Graywolf Press, 2000.

This book is a memoir/lyric essay told in the form of meditations triggered
by the author's antique postcard collection. The postcards appear in black and
white next to the texts they prompt, and the postcard pieces move out from
stories of the author's parents—damaged survivors of the second World
War—to his own childhood and finally his own parenthood: a journey
through time and places, which postcards represent, but with a sometimes
brutal realism that seems the opposite of postcard sentimentality.

White, E. B. "Afternoon of an American Boy." In *Essays of E. B. White*,
reprinted edition. New York: Perennial, 1999.

White's essay is a flawless piece of memoir: a personal reminiscence crafted
into a literary work that is neither self-indulgent nor limited. He captures the
awkwardness of early acquaintance between the sexes, escorting a girl he
admires to a tea-dance. At the same time he pokes nuanced fun at a scourge
of the mid-twentieth century, the House Un-American Activities Committee (HUAC), whose eventual chairman was the older brother of White's
teenage crush.

Williams, Terry Tempest. "The Clan of One-Breasted Women." In *Refuge: An Unnatural History of Family and Place*, second edition. New York: Vintage Books, 2001.

Williams opens this essay with a bold declaration—"I belong to a Clan of One-Breasted Women." It sounds grand, tribal, until we learn she is talking about coming from a lineage of women all of whom have undergone mastectomies. Williams's father reveals to her that her dreams of a flash in the desert are part of a real memory: that of seeing aboveground bomb testing in the 1950s. The fact of the testing, and the heavy fallout on Utah, is the chip of information Williams needs to question her family's high legacy of cancer.

Woolf, Virginia. "The Death of the Moth." In *The Death of the Moth and Other Essays*, reprinted edition. New York: Harcourt Brace Jovanovich, 1974.

This short, intensely poetic recounting of a moth's dying at the author's window is rich in connotations: the attempts to preserve a life through writing, as Woolf is doing, versus the "bead of pure life" that is the moth, flickering out in its brief and record-less existence.

Suggestions for Further Reading

Lopate, Phillip, ed., *The Art of the Personal Essay*. New York: Anchor Books, 1994.

An anthology of classic essays from antiquity to the twentieth century, providing an excellent historical overview of the form.

D'Agata, John, ed., *The Next American Essay*. St. Paul: Graywolf Press, 2003.

An anthology that takes up where Lopate's anthology leaves off, including experimental work that complicates the term "essay."

Root, Robert and Michael Steinberg, eds., *The Fourth Genre: Contemporary Writers of/on Creative Nonfiction.* Boston: Allyn and Bacon, 1999.

An excellent collection of essays by a variety of contemporary writers in the genre.

Kitchen, Judith and Mary Paumier Jones, eds., *In Short: A Collection of Brief Creative Nonfiction.* New York: W.W. Norton, 1996, and *In Brief: Short Takes on the Personal.* New York: W.W. Norton, 1999.

Both these volumes collect a wide array of "short-short" essays, providing the reader with a variety of approaches to the form.

Zinsser, William. *Inventing the Truth: The Art and Craft of Memoir.* Boston: Houghton Mifflin, 1987.

Interviews with several writers of memoir that elucidate some of the key issues that come up as soon as we begin to write in this genre.

Index